Feeding the Flock

Feeding the Flock

Martha McNatt

BETHANY HOUSE PUBLISHERS
MINNEAPOLIS, MINNESOTA 55438
A Division of Bethany Fellowship, Inc.

Published by Bethany House Publishers
A Division of Bethany Fellowship, Inc.
6820 Auto Club Road, Minneapolis, Minnesota 55438

Printed in the United States of America

Library of Congress Cataloging-in-Publication Data

McNatt, Martha
Feeding the flock.

Includes index.
1. Quantity cookery. I. Title.
TX820.M4 1987 661.5'7 87-717
ISBN 0-87123-956-6 (pbk.)

MARTHA McNATT is a food service professional with a strong church women's group involvement. Receiving a B.S. in Home Economics from the University of Tennessee, she spent fourteen years as the Director of Food Services and Nutrition of the Madison County Schools in Jackson, Tennessee. The developer of a 90-hour food service management curriculum used in school systems and community colleges for training school cafeteria workers, she also works as a free-lance consultant for women's church groups.

Contents

Introduction

Dear Reader:

Are you involved in a church congregation whose members enjoy eating together at church? Does your congregation often serve special-occasion banquets, holiday meals, women's luncheons, showers, receptions, and teas? Are your church women untrained in quantity food preparation? Does your church staff NOT include a Director of Food Services? If you answered yes to one or more of the above questions, this book is for you.

Preparing a meal in a church kitchen may be a totally frustrating experience. Often the kitchen is poorly equipped, with small and large utensils that were not made for each other. This book will suggest a minimum list of equipment needed to prepare meals successfully for fifty to two hundred persons.

Certain differences exist between quantity food purchasing techniques and supermarket buying. This book will outline the differences, and suggest advantages and disadvantages of each method. We will attempt to acquaint you with basic quantity food purchasing terminology, packaging sizes, and amounts to purchase for one hundred servings.

Often the most difficult part of meal preparation is determining the menu. Menus and recipes will be suggested for church functions in four categories: Regular Church Fellowship Dinners, Women's Luncheons, Holiday and Special Occasion Meals, and Meals for Kids of All Ages. Menu items and recipes may be mixed and matched for hundreds of menu combinations. A separate section will provide recipes from which menus may be planned for church parties, showers, receptions, and teas.

Preparation methods must be adjusted when preparing foods in quantity. Conversion of home-size recipes to quantity preparation may result in a poor product. All recipes included have been selected for ease of preparation, widespread appeal, and minimum equipment requirements.

Appointing a person to direct food preparation in your church is desirable, whether volunteer or paid, but if this arrangement does not exist, appointment should be made on a meal-to-meal basis. One person should be in charge of coordinating menu selection, purchasing, preparation, serving and cleanup.

Many people are afraid to attempt quantity food preparation, but the skills are easily mastered, and the experience may lead to a place of service in your church. Don't be intimidated by a hungry crowd of Christians. Enjoy!

Martha McNatt

Nutrition Standards

Nutritional Standards included in *Feeding the Flock* agree with recommendations by the United States Senate and the United States Department of Agriculture that Americans should reduce consumption of animal fats, salt, and sugar, and increase intake of fruits, vegetables, and complex carbohydrates. For this reason, certain recipe modifications have been made, including the following:

1. All recipes recommend the use of margarine instead of butter. Although vegetable fats burn at a lower temperature than animal fats, careful temperature control in sauteeing, and melting will achieve satisfactory results using margarine. Butter may be substituted for margarine if desired.
2. Salt has been reduced or eliminated from some recipes. Canned vegetables and fruits usually contain salt; therefore salt has been eliminated in recipes using these products. Additional salt may be added if desired.
3. Vegetable oils or shortenings are substituted for lard or animal fats for seasonings and pastries.
4. Whipped toppings are substituted for whipped cream. It should be noted that most whipped toppings contain coconut oil which may be unacceptable in fat reduction diet plans.
5. Whole grain breads are included in menu suggestions. Recipes for these breads can be found in the recipe section.
6. Use of raw fruits and vegetables is suggested, and menus include ideas for incorporating them into meal plans.
7. Portion size may be smaller than what some church cooks normally use. Portion sizes are specified with most recipes, and should be considered in individual use.
8. Lean ground beef is specified in some recipes. In most recipes using beef and pork, draining of excess fat is recommended.
9. The proportion of dessert recipes to other recipes is smaller in *Feeding the Flock* to encourage the use of fresh fruit desserts as widely as possible.
10. To maintain product quality, the amount of sugar has been reduced in most fruit-based desserts but not in cakes, cookies, and pies.

Purchasing Pointers

When purchasing food for a family, the purchaser considers quality, cost, family likes and dislikes, seasonal availability, packaging, ease of storage, and knowledge and skill of the person preparing the food. Most of these considerations affect the purchasing of food for a large group.

One additional consideration is necessary when buying food in large quantity. The purchaser must decide whether to purchase from the local supermarket or order from a quantity food vendor. There are advantages to both systems, but usually the advantages of purchasing basic supplies from a quantity food vendor outweigh the disadvantages. Advantages of buying from a quantity vendor include:

1. *Packaging*. A #10 can takes only a few seconds more to open than a supermarket-size can. One #10 replaces 4–6 supermarket-size cans. Bulk pack frozen foods and vegetables have the same advantage: only 1 package to open and dispose of. In the same manner, meats are packaged to save the consumer time and effort.

2. *Convenience*. A quantity food vendor will deliver the food you need to your church kitchen, usually within 48 hours of the time you place your order. A salesperson may call at the church, or your order will be accepted by phone.

3. *Availability*. A quantity food salesperson is accustomed to large orders. If you decide to buy at the supermarket, you may have to mix brands or shop in several different stores.

4. *Suitability of product*. Quantity food packers design a product line to provide items that would be labor prohibitive when prepared in large quantity. (Example: One packer provides a frozen fruit mix containing fresh peaches, grapes, and melon, which is delicious and relatively inexpensive—instant fruit salad without peeling, chopping or waste.)

5. *Special services available*. Most large packers develop recipes and suggestions tailored to preparing meals for large groups. If you ask your salesperson, he may have on hand information useful to you.

Some disadvantages do exist in purchasing from a quantity food vendor. Consider the following:

1. *The buyer does not see the product.* Normally, purchasing from a quantity food salesperson means ordering from a "book," that contains information about each product. The book will describe the product, grade, packaging size, price, and other specific information about the product. Purchasing may be done by phone. In either case, the purchaser must trust the vendor to provide the right product at the right cost, in the right amount, and deliver on a reliable schedule.

2. *Product substitutions.* Many food service companies are computerized. The computer is often programmed to substitute another product if the product ordered is out of stock—usually a brand or product equal to the one ordered. It may, however, be programmed to substitute a lower quality item. Careful inspection of the product delivered is important to insure quality.

3. *Full service may not be provided.* Except from large food vendors, certain items are usually not available from the quantity food salesperson. For example, you will probably need to purchase fresh fruits and vegetables from the supermarket or from a quantity produce vendor, even if you buy everything else from a quantity food vendor.

4. *Some items may be frozen instead of fresh.* Ground beef, for example, is almost always frozen in 15-pound blocks from your quantity vendor. A better choice may be family-size packs bought fresh at your supermarket.

5. *Price.* One widespread misconception is that buying from a quantity food vendor is buying wholesale. This is not true. While savings may be realized on some products, a quantity food vendor usually buys from a broker in the same manner that a retail grocer buys from a wholesaler.

An ideal situation may be to purchase food for your church dinner from a large supermarket that has a section for "institutional pack" foods. Many quantity food companies maintain a "cash and carry" department where you may purchase a product in institutional-size and broken-case lots.

After you have weighed the above considerations, you may want to get acquainted with your quantity food salesperson. Perhaps there is one in your congregation. The most important factor is finding a salesperson whose company is reliable, able to deliver as promised, quality oriented, and able to offer you the services you need.

Before purchasing food for any meal, the buyer needs the following information:

1. Menu to be served.
2. Foods on hand that may be used.
3. Approximate number to be served.
4. Equipment available for food preparation and serving.
5. Storage facilities.
6. Number of workers available and their skills.

Before buying food, the purchaser should analyze the recipes, listing ingredients needed to prepare each one. Foods on hand should be checked carefully. (No need to buy sugar if there is already half a dozen partially used bags in the kitchen.)

The next step is to determine how much of each item to buy. This may be the most difficult task for the inexperienced food purchaser. Most church meals are prepared with a budget in mind. Overproduction may result in unnecessarily high food costs, while underproduction may mean somebody doesn't eat. Following are some commonly used items (including items in recipes included in this book), with information which will assist the purchaser in arriving at the right quantity to purchase for 100 servings. Quantities that vary from 100 will need to be calculated mathematically. Example: For 150, multiply each item by 1.5.

FOOD AND TYPE	SERVING SIZE	AMOUNT FOR 100	OTHER INFORMATION
Ground Beef	3 ozs.	25 lbs.	
Beef Roast (boneless)	4 ozs.	40 lbs.	
Beef Roast (bone in)	4 ozs.	45 lbs.	
Beef or Pork Ribs	4 ozs.	90 lbs.	
Beef Steak (round)	4 ozs.	40 lbs.	
Beef for Stew	2½ ozs.	25 lbs.	
Beef, canned with gravy	2½ ozs.	9 #10	Usually packed 6 #10 cans per case
Pork Chops	2 small	Purchase by count	
Pork Sausage	2 1½ oz.-patties	20 lbs.	Available IQF* in 10 lb. packages.
Pork Roast	4 ozs.	60 lbs.	Bone In
Cured Ham	4 ozs.	40 lbs.	

*Individually quick frozen.

Frankfurters	1 2-ozs.	12 ½ lbs.	Usually packed 8 per package
Chicken Thighs	1	Purchase by count and weight	A wide choice available
Chicken Drumsticks	1	Purchase by count	
Chicken Breasts	1 piece		
Turkey	2 ozs.	60 lbs.	Four medium turkeys
Tuna (canned)	2 ozs.	18 lbs.	Use 4½ 4-lb. cans
Spaghetti Sauce, Canned	2 oz.	4 #10 cans	

Purchasing Fruits and Vegetables

If using canned fruits or vegetables, a simple guide to follow is that each #10 can will yield about 20 servings. Number-10 cans are usually packed 6 per case. A safe formula, particularly if men are being served, is to use 1 case for each 100 persons. Yield will vary according to package. Usually grade A fancy fruits and vegetables are packed tighter, therefore will yield more servings per can than lower grades. Grade B canned fruits and vegetables to be used in casseroles, stews, and cobblers are just as wholesome and are somewhat lower in price.

Vegetables—Fresh and Frozen

Mixed green salad is one of the most often-used menu items for church dinners. In the recipe section is a guide for preparing 100 1-cup servings.

Occasionally for a church function, it may be desirable to prepare fresh vegetables from scratch. Generally speaking, allow 20–25 pounds of ready-to-cook fresh vegetables for 100 servings. Example: Buy about 25 pounds of fresh green beans. For vegetables purchased in the shell (like lima beans), buy twice as many pounds as for ready-to-cook vegetables.

Fresh vegetables that vary from the above generalization include the following:

BROCCOLI—For one hundred ½ cups fresh cooked broccoli, buy 40 lbs.

CABBAGE—For one hundred ½ cups chopped or shredded cabbage, buy 12 pounds.

POTATOES—Because potatoes are heavier than most other vegetables, 30 pounds of fresh potatoes will be needed for 100 servings.

Purchasing Table for Fresh Fruits

Since fresh fruits are usually used in combination with other foods, the following table uses ⅓ cup as the basic serving size. Example: Apples, grapes, and peaches in the ⅓-cup serving size will produce one hundred generous servings of fruit salad.

FRUIT	AMOUNT TO PURCHASE FOR 100 SERVINGS
Apples	12 lbs.
Bananas	17 lbs.
Grapes	14 lbs.
Oranges	25 lbs.
Peaches	17 lbs.
Raisins	8 lbs.
Strawberries	9 qts.
Pineapple	¼ pineapple per serving

Purchasing Frozen Vegetables

For 100 servings of frozen vegetables, use the same guidelines as for fresh ready-to-cook vegetables. Most frozen vegetables may be purchased in two different pack styles: 20-pound bulk packages or cases of 6 or 8 smaller packages. Cases packed with 6 4-pound or 8 2½-pound packages usually cost a little more than the 20-pound bulk pack.

Purchasing Pasta Products

Spaghetti, macaroni, and noodles come in a wide variety of shapes and sizes. For a church supper, the choice is usually regular spaghetti. One pound of dry pasta will yield about 10 cups of cooked product. For 100 servings of spaghetti, macaroni, or noodles, purchase 15 pounds of dry product. From your quantity food vendor, pasta is usually available in 5-pound packages.

Steps in Planning, Purchasing, and Preparation

1. Plan the menu, considering the following: cost, equipment available, time, skill of workers, number of workers.
2. Develop a market list, deciding which items are to be purchased from a quantity food vendor, and which items from the supermarket. Make a list for each source.
3. Determine how much of each item to buy.
4. Place order with food vendor at least two days in advance of time needed.
5. Purchase fresh items as near as possible to time of use.
6. Identify equipment to be used and have it readily available if possible.
7. Develop a work schedule with approximate time each task should be started in order to finish before serving time.
8. Assign jobs to workers, making sure each understands what is to be done, how, and when.
9. Double check as preparation progresses. Everybody forgets something sometimes.

Equipment Needs

Knowing that many home-style appliances find their way into church kitchens, I do not wish to imply that yours must be a model of stainless steel equipment in order to serve effectively. There are, however, certain considerations which must be reviewed in order to prepare foods in quantity with any degree of ease. Consider the following:

1. The oven must be large enough to accommodate an 18 × 26-inch baking pan. (Most home-style range ovens are not.)
2. Surface burners must be sturdy enough to withstand the weight of a 12–20-quart cooking utensil. (Most home ranges are not so equipped.)
3. Refrigerators must contain shelving wide enough and deep enough to accommodate 12–20-quart containers. (Home refrigerators may have adjustable shelves, but lack space for adequate storage of foods needed.)
4. Beverage servers must be compact, fast, durable and sturdy.
5. An ice machine with adequate ice storage capacity should be conveniently located.
6. Dishwashing equipment needs will vary according to local usage. If disposable plates and bowls are used, home-style dishwashing equipment should serve adequately for washing flatware and glassware. Large-sized cooking utensils will not usually fit into home-style dishwashers. Several recommendations will follow for common dishwashing situations.
7. A minimum of 16 feet of counter work space per 100 meals should be available.
8. Mobile carts for transporting food and dishes must be available.
9. Some arrangement must be made for serving food and beverages.
10. Equipment for bussing and cleanup must be provided.

11. A method of thawing, warming, and preparing small quanitities of food is highly desirable.

With the above considerations in mind, the following list of basic equipment is recommended for preparing and serving a meal for 100 people.

1. One commercial range, either gas or electric, with oven at least 19 inches deep and 27 inches wide, with a minimum of 3 shelves. The range may be solid top or 6-burner.

Alternate I: One convection oven, gas or electric, with minimum dimensions stated above, with at least 8 racks. This oven to be used in combination with one home-style range.

Alternate II: A tilting braising pan to be used in combination with one convection oven. This equipment may be purchased on wheels and is extremely versatile in preparing main dish items. It operates like a home-style electric skillet, and is available in 30–60-quart capacity. This equipment is available in both gas and electric models. It is expensive and does not meet all food preparation requirements, but is worthy of consideration for a church kitchen.

2. One commercial refrigerator, capacity 47 cubic feet, equipped with one or two doors and constructed with stainless steel or bonded plastic over metal exterior and interior. A commercial refrigerator usually has no ice compartment, and is equipped with metal moveable shelves. A pass-through model is also available, with doors on both front and back if this is desirable in your kitchen arrangement. Note: Stainless steel exterior and interior models are very expensive, and if used only one or two days per week, are probably not cost efficient.

3. One ice machine with at least 60 pounds of ice-storage capacity. This machine may be an under-counter model or free standing and should be located in or near the dining area in order to facilitate traffic flow.

4. One commercial coffee maker with at least 3 12-cup pots. These machines are quick and efficient, and one unit may meet the hot beverage needs for 50–100 meals. They do require considerable attention, and beverage needs can be handled more comfortably if a commercial-size drip-style coffee maker is used in combination with the above described machine.

5. Dishwashing equipment needs vary with the style of service in any situation. For churches using all disposable plates, bowls, flatware, and glassware, no dishwashing equipment is necessary.

Cooking utensils will need to be washed by hand. Churches using disposable plates and bowls, but permanent glassware and flatware, usually find one or two home-style dishwashers adequate. Cooking utensils will need to be washed by hand since a home-style dishwashing machine will not operate efficiently if loaded with large cooking pots. Churches using all china and permanent flatware and glassware will need a commercial dishwasher. Many models are available from a totally manual, single tank door model to fully automatic models with conveyor belts, and prewashing equipment.

It is usually advisable to seek the help of a professional food service consultant to help determine local needs. Thousands of dollars may be invested in a dishwashing system that does not meet your church's needs.

6. Work surface units. If counters are built in, they should be covered with a nonporous, crack- and stain-resistant surface. No metal edging should be used since this provides a favorable environment for bacterial growth. Stainless steel tables come in standard lengths from 4–12 feet and may be equipped with under table storage bins, spice shelves, open or closed under table storage, above table racks for hanging utensils, and stainless steel or galvanized metal legs. Stainless steel tables are expensive, but will endure for generations, are easy to clean, and meet public health standards for food service operations.

7. Small equipment for food preparation.

NAME OF ITEM	# NEEDED	DESCRIPTION
18 × 26-inch baking pans	4	Heavy aluminum
12 × 20 × 4-inch pans	3	Stainless steel heavy gauge
12 × 20 × 2-inch pans	3	Stainless steel heavy gauge
Stock pot (12 qt.)	1	Heavy gauge aluminum
Stock pot (20 qt.)	1	Note: These are unnecessary if a braising pan and a convection oven are available.
Mixer (12-qt. commercial)	1	Should be equipped with a dough hook and grinding and chopping plates.
Sauce pans (2 qt.)	2	Useful for melting butter, boiling water, making sauce.
Knives (paring)	2	
Knives (butcher)	2	
Knives (French chef's)	1	

Pastry brushes	2	An inexpensive 2-inch paint brush serves adequately.
Spoons for mixing and serving	6	3 slotted, 3 solid
Scoops #8 and #16	1 each	Long handles preferred
Ladles #6 and #8	1 each	

Some type of slicing and chopping equipment is desirable. A heavy home-style food processor may be adequate for chopping. If a commercial-type food processor is needed, most restaurant supply stores offer an adequate machine that is relatively inexpensive. Mixer attachments perform some grinding and chopping, but are unsatisfactory for coarse chopping and for slicing. Commercial slicers are very expensive, considering their limited use. Small lightweight slicers may be available from a retail dealer, but usually are not satisfactory for slicing large amounts of meat.

A 20-quart stainless steel bowl is useful for mixing large amounts of any food. Stainless steel is easy to clean and does not absorb odors like a plastic bowl does. Covered plastic containers are useful for storing pre-prepared foods, staples, and leftovers. These are available from restaurant supply stores in many sizes and shapes.

8. Serving Equipment. Although not absolutely necessary, a simple serving counter with 3 heated serving wells and a 24-inch area for cold foods, will simplify the common problem of keeping foods hot and cold.

9. One heavy-duty stainless steel cart with 3 shelves may be adequate for transporting foods and soiled dishes to and from the dining area. Two or more additional carts are useful.

10. One tabletop mobile storage rack equipped with slides for 18 x 26-inch pans is a useful item of equipment, providing a place for holding rolls, or other foods after they are removed from the oven. One model is equipped with a cutting-board top, giving it double-duty potential.

11. One commercial-grade microwave oven is useful for thawing and for preparing small quantities of menu items, which may be necessary if food begins to run short.

Other pieces of commercial food service equipment may be useful. A convection steamer cooks foods quickly and without a pressure buildup. They are expensive, and persons unaccustomed to their operation, may avoid buying them. A church with a regular food service staff may find a convection steamer indispensable.

Safety Tips

1. BE CAREFUL—Most accidents are caused by carelessness.
2. Always use dry pot holders for handling hot pans. Never use an apron, towel, or dishcloth for a pot holder.
3. Open pots by raising the back side of the lid first, so that steam escapes away from your face and body.
4. Keep handles of pots and pans turned away from kitchen traffic aisles.
5. Do not fill kettles or pots too full.
6. Avoid allowing food or water to boil over.
7. Always stir with a long-handled spoon or paddle.
8. If food catches on fire, spread salt or baking soda on it. Never use water.
9. Remember, large quantities of food are heavy. Be sure you have a firm footing before attempting to lift a heavy pot.
10. Use a cart whenever possible to help you carry heavy loads.
11. Keep floors clean and dry. Wipe up spills immediately.
12. Wear low-heeled shoes with nonskid soles when working in a kitchen.
13. Always be alert and concentrate on your work when using a slicer or other unfamiliar equipment. Avoid unnecessary conversations when running this equipment.
14. Always unplug any equipment before cleaning.
15. Be sure your kitchen is equipped with a fire extinguisher.
16. Have fire department telephone numbers in a handy place near the telephone.

Kitchen Shortcuts

1. Cooking foods in serving pans whenever possible will save you time and labor.
2. Church kitchens often have more pans than covers. Aluminum foil makes an excellent tight cover.
3. Paper liners purchased in appropriate sizes for baking pans will save time and dishwashing.
4. Never use your hands to do a job that a machine can do quicker and better.
5. Always work with both hands, and try to shorten the distance hands must travel to do a job.
6. Tape a grocery bag to the edge of the table for waste paper, egg shells and other kitchen waste.
7. Make use of grinding and chopping equipment. Saves time and produces uniform results.
8. Measure dry ingredients before liquid ingredients to avoid unnecessary cleanup of measuring equipment.
9. Avoid handling dough whenever possible. Make dropped cookies instead of rolled ones, batter pastries instead of rolled pastry.
10. Chop foods such as celery, carrots or string beans in bunches rather than singly.
11. Use the largest possible measuring tool—a quart rather than four cups—a gallon rather than four quarts—a tablespoon rather than three teaspoons.
12. Always allow a butter cake to cool in the pan for 10–15 minutes. Turn out on a wire rack rather than a flat surface.
13. To decorate a cake without a decorator bag, cut the corner off an envelope, forcing the icing through the hole.
14. Use a wet knife to cut a fresh cake for a smoother cut.
15. Kitchen scissors are useful for cutting meats, herbs, vegetables, and cheese.
16. When baking potatoes, to cut time in half, boil for 15 minutes before starting oven time.

17. To revive limp celery, place in cold water and add a slice of raw potato.
18. Add a ½ cup of salt to the first water when washing fresh green vegetables. This will bring any worms to the surface.
19. Always keep a carton of baking soda in the church refrigerator to absorb odors.
20. The difference between a boil and a simmer is like the difference between a laugh and a smile. Simmer is moderate activity. Boil is more active.
21. Any dish that has contained eggs or starchy foods should be soaked in cold water, not hot.
22. If a baking recipe calls for melted shortening, always melt it in the baking pan you plan to use. Saves dishwashing.
23. Cool baked products away from drafts. Too much cool air may cause the product to fall.
24. A bread wrapper makes a satisfactory surface for rolling dough. Instant cleanup.
25. When a recipe calls for hard-cooked eggs, consider breaking them into a pan of water. Results are the same if eggs are to be used in combination with other foods. Saves peeling.

Hints for Recipe Variation

1. Baking powder biscuits are more flaky if flour and shortening are not too finely mixed.
2. Add chocolate mint patties to chocolate cake icing for a pleasing blend of flavors.
3. Combining vanilla flavoring with lemon or orange flavoring adds variety to cakes and icings.
4. A little vinegar added to boiled frosting will keep it from becoming brittle.
5. If cooked white frosting fails to set, add confectioners sugar until desired consistency is reached.
6. Add some chocolate chips to white frosting while it is hot. Tastes delicious.
7. Cookies or doughnuts may be sugared by tossing in a paper bag with sugar.
8. For a nice decoration on white frosting, use multicolored gum drops.
9. For a tastier apple pie, sprinkle grated cheese over the top during the last 15 minutes of baking time.
10. Try adding vanilla to fruit pies and cobblers.
11. A few capers do wonders for seafood and chicken salad.
12. Chopped apples add crispness and flavor to meat and vegetable salads.
13. An equal quantity of whipped topping added to mayonnaise gives a smoother and better-tasting salad dressing.
14. To stretch mayonnaise or salad dressing, add some pickle juice. Enhances flavor too.
15. For fluffier mashed potatoes, add a bit of baking powder.
16. If you accidentally oversalt vegetables, add a dash of sugar to modify the saltiness.

17. Chicken or beef bouillon cubes add flavor to boiled vegetables.
18. Try mint leaves or mint jelly as a seasoning for green peas.
19. To stretch scrambled eggs, without damaging flavor, add bread crumbs.
20. A touch of basil improves the flavor of any dish containing tomatoes.
21. In some recipes for spaghetti, the secret ingredient is dried mint leaves.
22. Thyme and sage are two herbs which improve the flavor of poultry dishes.
23. Add fresh dill weed or dill seed to potato salad for a different flavor.
24. Freshly ground black pepper adds twice as much flavor as pepper purchased already ground.
25. Add a dash of nutmeg to meat stews and casseroles for a new flavor experience.

Measurement Abbreviations

Teaspoon	t.
Tablespoon	T.
Pint	pt.
Quart	qt.
Gallon	gal.
Ounce	oz.
Pound	lb.
Number	#
Package	pkg.
Dozen	doz.

Measurement Equivalents

3 teaspoons . . . . 1 tablespoon
8 tablespoons . . . . ½ cup
16 tablespoons . . . . 1 cup
2 cups . . . . 1 pint
2 pints . . . . 1 quart
4 quarts . . . . 1 gallon

Common Scoop, Ladle, and Can Sizes

Number-8 scoop	½ cup
Number-16 scoop	¼ cup
Number-40 scoop	1½ tablespoons
Number-4 ladle	½ cup
Number-6 ladle	¾ cup
Number-8 ladle	1 cup
Number-16 ladle	1 pint
Number-303 can	2 cups
Number-2 can	2½ cups
Number-2½ can	3½ cups
Number-3 cylinder	5¾ cups
Number-10 can	12 cups

Smaller Can Equivalents to #10 Cans

Number-303 cans 7
Number-2 cans 5
Number-2½ cans 4
Number-3 cylinders 2

Oven Temperature Chart

Very slow oven	200–250 degrees F.
Slow oven	250–325 degrees F.
Moderate oven	325–400 degrees F.
Hot oven	400–500 degrees F.
Very hot oven	Above 500 degrees F.

Important Note: All oven temperatures specified are for conventional ovens. If a convection oven is used, temperatures suggested should be lowered by 50 degrees Fahrenheit.

Menus for One Hundred Servings

ALL-CHURCH FELLOWSHIP DINNERS

Spaghetti with Meat Sauce
Chef's Salad   Homemade Dressing
Texas Toast
Banana Pudding

All Saints Meat Loaf
Twice-Baked Potatoes   Marinated Green Beans
Hot Rolls
Peach Cobbler

Barbecue Beef or Pork
Baked Beans   Chips   Vinegar Slaw
Buns
Chocolate Ice-Box Pie

Oven-Fried Chicken
Green Peas in Potato Nest   Apple Rings
Iced Cake Squares

Country Fried Steak
Seasoned Rice   Copper Pennies
Hot Biscuits
Ice Cream with Chocolate Sauce

Stuffed Pork Chops
Hot Curried Fruit   Corn Pudding
Hot Rolls
Chocolate Brownies

Franks and Sauerkraut
Hot Potato Salad Corn on the Cob
Hot Rolls
Fruit Crisp

Lasagna
Lettuce Wedge Italian Dressing
Frozen Fruit Salad
Garlic Toast
Pound Cake

Barbecued Chicken
Escalloped Potatoes Raw Broccoli Salad
Hot Biscuits
Apple Cobbler

Pot Roast of Beef
Potatoes Carrots Onions
Ambrosia

Pork Sausage Patties with Apples
Vegetable Medley
Whole Wheat Rolls
Peach Delight

Pepper Steak
Frozen Green Peas with Peppers and Mushrooms
Parsley Potatoes
Cloverleaf Rolls
Fruit Gelatin and Cookies

Chicken Tetrazzini
Spiced Peach Halves English Pea Salad
Toasted Rolls
Strawberry Shortcake

Chicken Pot Pie with Biscuit Topping
Rosy Pear Salad
Hot Biscuits
Raisin-Rice Pudding

White Beans with Ham Hock
Seasoned Turnip Greens   Confetti Corn
Pickled Beets with Onion Rings
Corn Bread Squares
Ice Cream Bars

Hearty Beef Vegetable Soup
Mexican Corn Bread
Assorted Fresh Fruits
Oatmeal Cookies

Creamed Turkey on Corn Bread
Green Beans with Almonds   Candied Yams
Corn Bread
Prune Squares

Salmon Croquettes with Cream Sauce
Macaroni and Cheese   Lemon Buttered Broccoli
Rolls
Fruit Gelatin with Bananas

Mexican Casserole with Corn-Bread Topping
Mixed Green Salad with Tomatoes
Toasted Hard Rolls
Ice Cream and Cookies

Corned Beef and Cabbage
Buttered Minted Carrots   Southern Potato Salad
Corn Muffins
Bread Pudding

HOLIDAY AND SPECIAL-OCCASION MEALS

CELEBRATING THE NEW YEAR

Ham and Biscuits   Hoppin John
Layered Vegetable Salad
Corn Relish   Escalloped Tomatoes
Biscuits
Apple Pie

VALENTINE BANQUET

Stuffed Chicken Breast
Sweetheart Parslied Potatoes   Seasoned Green Beans
Rosy Apple Rings
Angel Biscuits
Red Velvet Cake

ATHLETIC BANQUET

Big-Team Barbecued Beef Brisket
High-Scoring Beans   Hero Slaw
Assorted Chips   Buns
Victory Chess Pie

HOMECOMING BUFFET

Boiled Tennessee Country Ham
Chicken and Dumplings
Grandma's Fried Apples   Farm-Fresh Vegetables
Raisin-Rice Pudding
Chocolate Cake

EASTER MORNING BUFFET

Creamed Eggs on Toasted English Muffins
Tiny Oven-Cooked Link Sausages
Hot Curried Fruit
Hot Cinnamon Rolls

INTERNATIONAL OR MISSIONS BANQUET

Oriental Beef or Pork on Rice
French Style Green Beans   Candied African Yams
Monkey Bread
Black Forest Cake

PATRIOTIC BANQUET

Cider Baked Virginia Ham with New England Cranberry Relish
Williamsburg Ratatouille   Stuffed Yellow Squash
Indian Corn Sticks   Kentucky Rolls
Georgia Sweet Potato Pie

SENIOR CITIZENS BANQUET

Baked Chicken Breast on Bed of Rice
Whole Baked Stuffed Apple
Frozen Green Peas with Onions
Hot Rolls
Chocolate Ice-Box Pie

ALL-CHURCH STEW SUPPER

Deacons Stew
Texas Toast   Assorted Crackers
Bring a Dessert

THANKSGIVING DINNER

Sliced Turkey with Dressing and Gravy
Cranberry Sauce
Baked Asparagus with Almonds
Yellow Squash Casserole
Raw Vegetables and Dip
Cloverleaf Rolls
Rainbow Cake

CELEBRATING CHRISTMAS

Turkey and Dressing Casserole
Broccoli Spears with Curry Sauce
Orange-Glazed Carrots
Frozen Cherry Salad
Crescent Rolls
Sugar-Plum Pudding

Recipes for One Hundred Servings

BEEF OR PORK

Barbecued Beef or Pork

Barbecue is available prepared by professional barbecue cooks in many sections of the country. It may be purchased boneless by the pound or in whole shoulders or briskets. Some saving may be realized by purchasing barbecue in large pieces and boning the meat yourself. In some barbecue, especially pork, there is substantial waste. Boning and chopping is a time-consuming process. Pre-boned and chopped all-lean pork barbecue is expensive.

Several institutional packers are offering frozen beef or pork barbecue in 5-pound containers. Although less flavorful than fresh barbecue, it is very acceptable for quantity meals and it saves labor and time. Allow 3–5 ounces of frozen barbecue per serving.

Many versions of barbecue from ground beef are available, usually based upon regional preference. The following page gives one example.

Midwestern Barbecue

15 pounds ground beef
10 green peppers
6 medium onions
1 cup vinegar
½ cup salt
1 cup brown sugar
3 tablespoons garlic powder
2 #10 cans tomato catsup

Brown ground beef with vegetables and seasonings. Add catsup and simmer until mixture is very thick. Serve on a bun with a #8 scoop.

Corned Beef and Cabbage

20–25 pounds prepared corned beef brisket
13 medium heads cabbage

Prepare corned beef briskets according to package directions in two pans. When meat is done, cut cabbage heads into 8 wedges each. Gently place cabbage wedges on top of beef briskets. Cover pans tightly and steam cabbage for 20 minutes in oven (or until wedges are tender). Slice beef and serve 1 cabbage wedge and 1 slice of beef.

Barbecued Beef Brisket

Buy 20–25 pounds of boneless beef brisket. Trim away any excess fat. Season brisket with salt. Place in 2 pans and bake uncovered in oven at 325° for 1½ hours, fat side up. Turn briskets and cover with your favorite pre-prepared barbecue sauce. Cook an additional 1½ hours until briskets are tender, basting frequently with drippings and sauce. Slice diagonally across the grain of the meat.

Oriental Beef (or Pork) with Rice and Vegetables

NOTE: Tilting braising pan or other large container is essential.

20 pounds boneless beef or pork cut into 1-inch cubes
1 quart stock (or 8 boullion cubes dissolved in 1 qt. water)
1 cup oriental stir-fry seasoning mix
4 cups cooking oil
1 quart onion, chopped
1 quart celery, chopped
1 pound fresh mushrooms, sliced
20 pounds frozen oriental vegetables

Brown meat cubes in oil. Add onions and celery and stir fry until crisp tender. Push beef and vegetables to back of pan. Add stock and seasonings to drippings in pan. Mix well and add frozen vegetables. Stir fry for 2–3 minutes, then mix in beef and other vegetables. Serve over bed of rice.

Oven-Cooked Rice

6 pounds uncooked rice
2 tablespoons salt
3 gallons boiling water
6 tablespoons cooking oil

Into each of 2 12 × 20 × 4-inch pans, place 3 pounds uncooked rice. Add salt to boiling water and pour 1½ gallons into each pan. Stir only enough to distribute rice evenly in pans. Add 3 tablespoons cooking oil to each pan to prevent foaming. Cover or foil pans tightly and cook in oven at 350° for 30–35 minutes. Do not remove cover for 5–10 minutes after removing from oven. Fluff with long-tined fork if desired.

Country Steak with Gravy — 3 18 × 26-inch pans

25 pounds ground beef
4 cups flour
¼ cup salt
1 tablespoon black pepper

Mix flour, salt, and pepper, sprinkling three pans generously with this mixture. Portion ground beef with a #8 scoop. Sprinkle top with another layer of flour mixture and press down firmly, allowing portion lines to show. Cook in oven at 350° for about 20 minutes or until lightly brown. Drain and use drippings to make brown gravy.

Brown Gravy

Make a roux, using 1 cup beef drippings and 2 cups all-purpose flour. Allow this mixture to brown; then gradually add 5 cups water and stir until mixture thickens. Pour over country steak in pans or spoon over portions as served. For thinner gravy, increase water until desired thickness is reached.

Country Fried Round Steak

30 pounds round of beef or supermarket cut round steak
½ cup salt
2 tablespoons black pepper
3 tablespoons paprika
2 tablespoons garlic powder
8 cups flour
cooking oil for pan frying

Cut round steak into 4–5 ounce portions. Mix flour and seasonings. Dredge steak in flour mixture and pan fry in about ¾-inch deep cooking oil until surface is golden brown. Add 2 quarts of water to each pan and cover tightly. Cook in oven at 350° for 45 minutes or until steak is tender.

VARIATION: Pepper Steak–

Follow above directions with the following variations. Instead of adding water to pans, add one #10 can of tomatoes to each pan. Also add 2 cups chopped onion and 3 cups chopped green pepper to each pan before cooking in oven.

Lasagna — 96 2 × 4-inch servings

10 pounds ground beef
¼ cup salt
1 tablespoon black pepper
3 cups onion chopped
1 #10 can tomato sauce
1 #10 can water
½ cup sugar
¼ cup Worcestershire sauce
2 tablespoons garlic powder
4 pounds cottage cheese
2 pounds mild cheddar cheese
4 pounds lasagna noodles (uncooked)

Season meat with salt and pepper. Brown meat and onions lightly and drain. Add tomato sauce, water, and seasonings to meat mixture and simmer 25–30 minutes to blend flavors. Add cottage cheese to meat mixture and mix lightly. Layer as follows: Layer 1—one-quart meat-cheese mixture in each pan; layer 2—raw lasagna noodles, 8 per pan; layer 3—thin layer of shredded cheddar cheese. Repeat layering. Top with cheddar cheese (or you may substitute mozzarella). Cover pans tightly and bake in oven at 350° for 1 hour. Allow to stand for 15 minutes for easier portioning.

Meat Sauce for Spaghetti

15 pounds ground beef
6 large onions, chopped
1 medium stalk celery, chopped
4 #10 cans prepared spaghetti sauce

Divide ingredients in half. Cook each half in separate containers. Brown ground beef, onions, and celery until beef changes color. Drain off excess fat. Add spaghetti sauce and simmer for 45 minutes.

Spaghetti — 1-cup servings

15 pounds dry spaghetti
3 gallons water in each of two 12-quart stock pots
½ cup cooking oil in each pot
½ cup salt in each pot

Bring water to a boil. Add spaghetti slowly, allowing water to continue boiling. Be sure all surfaces of spaghetti are wet to prevent sticking. Cook at fast boil for approximately 9 minutes. Drain. Pour into pans containing spaghetti sauce and mix lightly. Serve at once.

Pot Roast of Beef

30 pounds beef pot roast
¼ cup salt
1 tablespoon black pepper
12 medium onions, quartered
8 bay leaves
¾ cup vinegar

Season roasts with salt and pepper and brown on all sides. Drain off drippings and save for gravy. Add onions, bay leaves, and water. Cover tightly. Cook in oven at 300° for 3 hours or until roasts are tender. Make gravy as directed for Country Steak. Slice roast into 3–4-ounce portions and serve with gravy as desired.

Savory Meat Loaf

25 pounds ground beef
½ cup salt
1 16-ounce loaf of bread, crumbled
1 quart milk
24 fresh eggs
5 pounds hot pork sausage
8 medium onions, chopped
1 medium stalk celery, chopped
1 quart tomato sauce

Mix together beef, salt, bread crumbs that have been soaked in milk and eggs. Brown pork sausage with celery and onions and drain excess fat. Mix with beef. Shape into loaves approximately 4 × 12 inches. Place 5 loaves into each of 2 12 × 20-inch pans. Top with tomato sauce. Bake at 325° for 1 hour. Yield: 10 servings per loaf.

VARIATION: Meat Balls

Shape meat mixture into generous meat balls (app. 5 per lb). Cook as above, reducing cooking time to 45 minutes. Serving size: one meat ball.

CHICKEN AND TURKEY DISHES

Barbecued Chicken

Select individual chicken pieces as desired, allowing about 25 pounds of breast or thighs for 100 servings. Place raw chicken pieces in 12 × 20 × 2-inch pans. Cover with prepared barbecue sauce or make your own. Bake at 350° for 1–1½ hours until pieces are browned and tender.

Barbecue Sauce for Chicken

1½ pounds flour
1 quart cooking oil
2 cups chopped onion
2 tablespoons black pepper
½ cup Worcestershire sauce
1 #10 can tomato catsup
1 pound brown sugar

Combine all ingredients and simmer for 30 minutes. Pour hot sauce over chicken and bake as directed above.

Chicken Pot Pie with Biscuit Topping

4 #10 cans mixed vegetables
2 cups finely chopped onion
2 cups finely chopped celery
1 cup plain flour
2 quarts chicken stock
¼ cup seasoned salt
2 tablespoons dry poultry seasoning or sage
5 pounds deboned chicken meat (use 10 pounds raw chicken)
6 cans biscuits (layered biscuits are best)

Pour 2 cans mixed vegetables, undrained, into each of 2 12 × 20 × 2-

inch pans. Add raw celery, onion, and seasonings. Thicken two quarts chicken stock with the flour and add to vegetables in pans. Place cooked deboned chicken meat on top of the vegetables. Separate biscuits into two layers, 60 per pan, and place on top of chicken and vegetables. Bake for 25 minutes at 350° or until biscuits are golden brown.

NOTE: Celery and onion will be crisp tender. Serve 2 biscuit halves, with meat and vegetables, per person. Additional hot biscuits are suggested as an accompaniment.

Chicken Tetrazzini

4 gallons chicken stock (use stock from cooking chicken, adding water if necessary to make 4 gals.)
10 pounds dry spaghetti cooked in above stock
10 pounds chicken meat cooked, deboned and diced
2 cups finely chopped onion
1 cup finely chopped green pepper
1 cup finely chopped red pepper
4 cups chopped celery
1 #10 can cream of mushroom soup
5 pounds shredded cheese

Drain the cooked spaghetti and save the stock. Add onions, peppers, celery, and mushroom soup to stock and simmer while performing the following step. Mix the meat with the spaghetti in 2 12×20×4-inch pans. Pour the stock mixture over the spaghetti-chicken mixture and top with shredded cheese. Bake in oven at 350° for about 30 minutes or until cheese is melted and casserole is bubbly.

VARIATION:

1. Turkey Tetrazzini—substitute turkey for chicken.
2. Tuna Tetrazzini—substitute tuna for chicken.

Oven-Fried Chicken

25 pounds chicken breasts or thighs
3 pounds melted margarine
3 pounds flour
¼ cup salt
2 tablespoons black pepper

Dip individual pieces of chicken in melted margarine then dredge in flour that has been seasoned with the salt and pepper. Place chicken pieces close together in baking pans. Cook in oven at 400° for 45 minutes to 1 hour or until surface is golden brown and chicken is tender. Do not turn.

NOTE: For oven frying, select 4-ounce breasts or thighs, which may be purchased from quantity food suppliers individually quick frozen and sized to customer's desires. Thaw in refrigerator for 24–48 hours. Cooking time will be longer if chicken is not completely thawed.

Creamed Turkey on Corn-Bread Squares

1 large turkey, cooked and deboned
1 gallon turkey broth
2 cups chopped green pepper
2 cups chopped red pepper
3 cups chopped onion
1 cup turkey fat
1 pound flour
¼ cup salt
1 gallon milk

Cook onions and peppers in turkey broth until tender. Make a roux with turkey fat, flour, and salt. Add turkey broth mixture and milk and stir over low heat until mixture thickens. Do not boil. Add turkey meat to sauce and allow to simmer until turkey and sauce are hot. Serve with a #6 ladle (¾ c.) over a 3 × 3-inch square of corn bread, which has been sliced and opened.

Corn Bread

6 cups self-rising flour
6 cups self-rising cornmeal (yellow or white as desired)
2 cups sugar
2 cups nonfat dry milk powder
24 eggs
3 cups cooking oil
10 cups water

Mix dry ingredients. Blend eggs, oil, and water together and add to dry ingredients, mixing well. Cook in 4 12 × 20 × 2-inch pans that have been greased and heated in the oven. Bake at 450° for 20 minutes or until golden brown.

Stuffed Chicken Breast

100 chicken breast halves, deboned
100 slices dried beef
100 slices bacon (about 6 lbs.)
3 quarts sour cream
1 #10 can mushroom soup
1 #10 can water

Place chicken breasts skin side down and top each with a slice of dried beef. Wrap a bacon slice around dried beef and chicken and arrange in baking pans skin side up. Combine sour cream, soup, and water and pour over chicken breasts. Bake in oven at 275° for 3 hours. Serve garnished with a sprig of fresh parsley.

Chicken and Dumplings

25 pounds cut up chicken pieces as desired
1 stalk celery, chopped, including leaves
3 tablespoons salt
1 tablespoon black pepper
8 cans biscuits
2 tablespoons parsley flakes

Cook chicken and chopped celery in enough water to cover. Save stock. Remove chicken pieces and bone, discarding skin. Add seasonings to stock and bring the liquid to simmering temperature. Pinch biscuits into 3 or 4 pieces and drop into simmering chicken stock. Cook until dumplings are sticky and set. Pour into 2 serving pans and gently add chicken. Sprinkle parsley on top of chicken and dumplings. Dumplings should thicken the chicken stock and absorb most of the liquid.

Creamed Eggs on English Muffins

60 hard-cooked eggs, chopped
2 cups margarine
1 quart flour
2½ gallons milk
1 tablespoon salt
1 teaspoon black pepper
½ cup Worcestershire sauce
50 English muffins split and toasted

Make a roux with melted margarine and flour. Slowly stir in milk until thickened to desired consistency. Add seasonings and chopped hard-cooked eggs. Serve over toasted English muffin halves.

NOTE: Hard-cooked eggs may be purchased ready to use from quantity food vendors.

Sliced Turkey with Dressing and Gravy

2 large turkeys (20 lbs. or more) cooked and sliced
3 gallons turkey stock (2 gals. for dressing—1 gal. for gravy). Add water if necessary to make this quantity
2 quarts chopped celery
4 quarts chopped onion
2 cups margarine
5 gallons bread crumbs (corn bread, white bread or commercially prepared stuffing mix)
½ cup sage, crumbled
2 tablespoons salt
1 tablespoon black pepper
18 eggs, beaten

Sauté celery and onion in margarine. Combine bread crumbs and seasonings. Add onions, celery, and enough stock to make a thick batter. (Start with 1 gal. and add as necessary.) Add eggs and mix well. Portion into 2 well-greased 12×20×2-inch pans (about 1½ gals. per pan). Bake at 350° for about 45 minutes to 1 hour. Serve with a #8 scoop (½ c.) topped with a slice of turkey. Gravy may be spooned over turkey and dressing or served as an accompaniment.

Turkey Gravy **2 tablespoons each serving**

Cook turkey necks, gizzards, and livers in ½ gallon water
1½ cups flour
1 tablespoon salt
1 teaspoon black pepper
4 tablespoons lemon juice (optional)
12 hard-cooked eggs

Remove giblets from water and cool. Mix flour with cooled stock and add reserved stock from turkey to make 1 gallon. Chop giblets, discarding grissle and bone. Add giblets and seasonings to stock and heat to simmering stage. Add chopped eggs and simmer until gravy is thickened.

NOTE: Adding lemon juice to gravy is a regional tradition in certain areas of the South.

Turkey and Dressing Casserole

NOTE: This recipe is made from 3 ingredients: turkey, dressing, and sauce. Directions for each are separated.

Turkey

2 medium-sized turkeys (12–15 lbs.)

Cook and debone turkeys. Pull or chop meat into bite-size pieces. Reserve stock.

Dressing Mix

5 gallons bread crumbs (reserve 4 qts. and drizzle about 1 lb. melted margarine over reserved crumbs)
¼ cup sage
1 stalk celery, chopped, including leaves
6 large onions, chopped

Cook onion and celery in 1 gallon of water. Add water and cooked vegetables to bread crumbs. Add sage. Mixture will be part moist, part dry.

Sauce

2 cups margarine
2 cups flour
2½ gallons turkey broth (adding water if necessary to reserved stock)
24 eggs, beaten

Make a roux of margarine and flour. Add turkey broth, eggs, and cook until thick. Allow to cool.

Mix casserole in 4 greased 12 × 20 × 2-inch pans in layers as follows: (1) dressing mix, (2) meat, (3) sauce. Repeat, ending with sauce. Bake for 30 minutes at 350°. Remove from oven and cover with buttered crumbs. Bake 15–20 minutes more or until crumbs are brown and crisp.

PORK DISHES

Pork Sausage Patties with Apples

200 pork sausage patties 1½ ounces
4 #10 cans cooking apples, unsweetened
½ cup cornstarch
Red food color as desired

Layer sausage patties in 12 × 20-inch pans and cook in oven at 350° until patties begin to brown. Drain excess fat. Drain apples and add red food coloring to juice if desired. Add cornstarch to liquid from one can of apples and stir until dissolved. Pour apples into pans of sausage patties. Pour thickened juice over apples. If more liquid is needed, use juice from apples. Return pans to oven. Cook until liquid is thickened and clear. Serve 2 patties and ½ cup of apples.

Stuffed Pork Chops

100 large lean pork chops
4 quarts sage-flavored stuffing mix
3 quarts boiling water
½ cup instant chicken bouillion granules or 12 cubes
2 cups chopped onion
2 cups chopped celery
6 eggs

Place pork chops in 2 lightly greased 18 × 26-inch baking pans. Dissolve bouillion in boiling water. Add to stuffing mix. Mix in celery, onion and eggs. Mix well. Use just enough liquid to make mixture stick together and hold its shape. Portion stuffing with a #30 scoop onto each chop. Bake in a slow oven at 325° for 1 hour.

Baked Ham Slices

25 slices smoked ham ¾-inch thick
(each slice cut into 4 pieces)
3 cups brown sugar
3 cups dried bread crumbs
½ cup dry mustard
3 cups orange juice
6 oranges, sliced crosswise
Whole cloves

Arrange ham in 2 12×20×2-inch pans. Insert whole cloves randomly into ham pieces. Mix sugar, bread crumbs and mustard and sprinkle over ham. Arrange orange slices over crumb mixture. Pour orange juice around edges of pans. Bake in oven at 350° for 40 minutes. Serve garnished with a maraschino cherry.

Boiled Country Ham

Ham which has been salt-cured and smoked is a Southern tradition that has gained nationwide popularity. The following directions for boiling a country ham are adapted from an old Tennessee recipe.

1. Cut off hock. Clean whole ham thoroughly with a brush or rough cloth. Trim off any dark, dry edges and discolored fat. Soak ham in cold water for 12 hours before cooking.
2. Fill large roaster about half full of water, putting ham in water, skin side up. Cover and place in oven at 450°. When water boils, reduce heat to 300° and cook 30 minutes per pound.
3. Allow to cool in juice for 4 or 5 hours.
4. Trim off skin and fat and slice with a sharp knife.
5. Serve sandwich style on hot biscuits, or serve cold as a main dish.

MISCELLANEOUS MAIN DISHES

Hearty Vegetable Soup with Beef and Chicken

3 #10 cans mixed vegetables
2 #10 cans tomatoes
1 #10 can whole kernel corn
1 #10 can lima beans
5 pounds fresh potatoes (or 1 #10 can tiny whole potatoes)
6 large onions, chopped
6 large green peppers, chopped
1 stalk celery, chopped
5 pounds ground chuck
1 large hen, cooked and deboned
Stock from cooking hen
¼ cup dried basil
¼ cup dried thyme

Mix vegetables in a 20-quart stock pot. Bring to a boil. Add seasonings. Brown ground chuck and add to soup pot. Add meat from hen and stock. Simmer on low heat for 1½ hours. Water may be added if thinner soup is desired.

NOTE: Soup stock will be clear. If more creamy stock is desired, substitute cream style corn for whole kernel corn.

Franks and Sauerkraut

100 1½ or 2 ounce frankfurters
4 #10 cans sauerkraut, drained
½ cup flour
2 quarts sauerkraut liquid

Chop franks into bite-size portions. Spread in 2 12 × 20 × 4-inch pans. Cover with sauerkraut. Blend flour with 1 quart of sauerkraut liquid and pour over franks and sauerkraut in pans. Cover pans and cook in oven at 350° for 45 minutes, or until franks are hot and puffy and sauerkraut is heated through. Serve ½ cup sauerkraut and the equivalent to 1 frankfurter.

Mexican Casserole with Corn-Bread Topping

15 pounds ground beef
6 large onions, chopped
1 #10 can tomatoes
⅓ cup chili powder
¼ cup salt
2 #10 cans whole kernel corn

Brown ground beef and onion in serving pans. Drain. Add other ingredients and simmer while corn bread is mixed.

Corn-Bread Topping

1 2-pound bag yellow self-rising cornmeal
1 2-pound bag self-rising flour
1 cup sugar
12 large eggs
1 cup vegetable oil
3 quarts milk

Combine dry ingredients in mixer for 3 minutes on low speed. Add other ingredients and mix thoroughly on low speed. Do not beat. Batter should be thinner than regular corn-bread batter.

Pour batter over pans of beef mixture and bake at 450° for 20–25 minutes or until golden brown. Serve ¾ cup beef mixture and 2 × 2-inch serving of corn bread.

Salmon Croquettes with Cream Sauce

4 64-ounce cans salmon (including liquid)
1 gallon cracker crumbs or dry bread crumbs
1 cup lemon juice
12 large eggs
Milk as necessary to mix

Combine all ingredients except milk in mixer. Mix, adding milk as necessary to bring mixture to consistency that will form into croquettes and hold its shape. Portion onto 2 lightly greased 18 × 26-inch baking sheet, using a #16 scoop. Bake at 350° for 30 minutes or until golden brown. Serve one croquette with cream sauce.

Cream Sauce

2 pounds melted margarine
2 quarts finely chopped celery, precooked tender
1½ cups flour
3 tablespoons salt
5 quarts milk

Combine flour, salt and margarine. Add milk and stir over low heat until mixture thickens. (Do not boil.) Add cooked celery. Serve 1 tablespoon of sauce over each croquette.

White Beans and Ham ¾-cup servings

10 pounds dry beans (Great Northern, Navy, or Lima)
¼ cup salt
4 gallons boiling water
5 pounds cooked ham, chopped into 1-inch chunks

Wash beans, discarding discolored or broken beans. Bring water to boil in 20-quart stock pot. Add beans and salt. Cover and set aside to soak for at least one hour. (Three or four hours is best.) After soaking, reheat in soaking water, and cook for 1½-2 hours or until beans are tender. After about ½ of the cooking time, add the ham chunks. Add water as needed if the beans become dry.

VARIATION: For easier preparation, use 6 #10 cans dried beans. Add the ham at beginning of preparation time. Simmer over low heat for 45 minutes to 1 hour.

Deacons Stew

3 large chickens, boiled and deboned
3 pounds stew beef, cut in 1-inch cubes
3 pounds wild game meat, cooked and deboned (squirrel, rabbit, deer)
1 #10 can green peas
1 #10 can whole kernel corn
1 #10 can lima beans
4 #10 cans tomatoes
4 #10 cans mixed vegetables
18 medium onions, chopped
12 large white potatoes, peeled and chopped
½ cup Worcestershire sauce
¼ cup salt
3 tablespoons garlic powder
Hot peppers as desired

Mix all ingredients (including broth from cooking meats) in a 30-quart stock pot. Cook over low heat until very thick (6 to 8 hours) stirring often. May be cooked outside in a 30-quart kettle.

FRUITS AND VEGETABLES

Fried Apples — ½-cup servings

4 #10 cans cooking apples
1 tablespoon red food coloring
1 pound margarine
8 cups sugar

Mix all ingredients and cook on top of range until liquid has condensed into a thick syrup and apple chunks appear shiny and coated with syrup.

Stuffed Apples — ½-cup servings

5 #10 cans whole apples (average 20 per can)
1 8-ounce package cinnamon candy bits
2 pounds white raisins, plumped in water for 10 minutes
1 16 oz. bag of miniature marshmallows

Carefully place whole apples in 12 × 20 × 2-inch pans, and heat in oven at 350° for 15 minutes or until apples are heated through. Mix marshmallows, raisins, and cinnamon candies and stuff apples with the mixture. Turn oven off and allow stuffed apples to stand until marshmallows and candies are partially melted. Serve warm, or chill and serve cold.

Asparagus with Almonds ½-cup servings

4 #10 cans cut asparagus, drained (reserve liquid)
12 hard-cooked eggs, sliced crosswise
1 3-pound can slivered almonds
3 pounds shredded cheese
1 #10 can celery soup
1 1-pound box round snack crackers, crushed

Place drained asparagus in 2 12 × 20 × 2-inch pans. Layer with eggs, almonds, and cheese. Cover with soup, adding reserved asparagus liquid if necessary. Cover with crumbs. Bake at 350° or until bubbly and lightly browned.

Seasoned Green Beans ½-cup servings

5 #10 cans French style green beans
2 cups chopped red sweet pepper
3 tablespoons garlic flavored salt

Season beans and simmer for 15 minutes. Serve hot.

Broccoli with Curry Sauce ½-cup servings

20 pounds fresh or frozen broccoli spears
2 tablespoons salt

Prepare in small amount of water. Cook until crisp tender. Drain.

Curry Sauce

1 quart mayonnaise
2 tablespoons curry powder
½ cup prepared mustard
2 cups sweet pickle juice
1 teaspoon hot pepper sauce

Mix and chill. Serve over broccoli or other vegetables.

Orange-Glazed Carrots ½-cup servings

5 #10 cans whole carrots (or 20 lbs. fresh carrots cooked)
2 pounds brown sugar
1 quart corn syrup
1 12-ounce can frozen orange juice concentrate
1 pound margarine

Place carrots (including liquid) into 2 12×20×2-inch pans. Mix sugar, syrup, and orange concentrate and coat carrots with this mixture. Dot with margarine and cook at 350° for 40 minutes, basting carrots twice during cooking time.

Corn Relish ¼-cup servings

2 #10 cans yellow whole kernel corn
2 cups chopped green peppers
2 cups chopped red sweet peppers
2 cups chopped onion

Mix all ingredients and marinate for several hours before serving.

Marinade for Vegetables

1 pint vegetable oil
1 pint vinegar
4 cups sugar
2 tablespoons celery seed

Mix and pour over drained vegetables.

NOTE: May be used over a wide variety of vegetables, including green beans, black-eyed peas, frozen green peas, beets, or combinations of vegetables. Keeps well in refrigerator for several days.

New England Cranberry Relish — 2T. per serving

3 pounds fresh cranberries
12 fresh oranges, peeled, seeded and sectioned
6 cups sugar

Wash cranberries and chop in food processor, being careful not to overprocess. Chop orange sections and add to cranberries. Add sugar, cover and chill.

Spiced Apple Rings — ¼-cup servings

2 #10 cans spiced apple rings

Chill cans. Open and drain. Serve 4–5 slices on each plate. No other preparation necessary.

Baked Beans — ¾-cup servings

6 #10 cans pork and beans
6 large onions, chopped
6 large green peppers, chopped (or 2 c. canned peppers)
1 pound brown sugar
2 quarts tomato catsup
1 cup prepared mustard
1 quart dark corn syrup
1 pound bacon

Combine all ingredients except bacon. Mix and place in 2 12 × 20 × 4-inch pans. Arrange bacon slices on top of bean mixture. Bake in oven at 350° for 50 minutes.

Green Beans with Almonds — ¾-cup servings

6 #10 cans French cut green beans
1 64-ounce can slivered almonds
3 pounds margarine

Place 3 cans of beans in each of two 12 × 20 × 4-inch pans. Top each pan with 3 cups margarine. Sprinkle slivered almonds liberally over green beans. Cook in oven at 350° for 45 minutes or until beans are hot and almonds are toasty.

Marinated Green Beans — ¾-cup servings

6 cans French cut green beans
1 16-ounce can chopped pimiento
1 quart vegetable oil
1 quart vinegar
4 cups sugar
½ cup celery seed

Drain the beans. Place 3 cans of beans in each of 2 12 × 20 × 4-inch pans. Add 8 ounces pimiento to each pan. Mix oil, vinegar, sugar and celery seed. Pour over green beans and stir well. Cover pans and refrigerate for several hours before serving. Serve cold.

Lemon-Buttered Broccoli Spears — 2–3 spears

1 20-pound bag frozen broccoli spears
6 quarts boiling water
3 pounds margarine
1 quart lemon juice

Bring water to boil in 20-quart stock pot. Drop broccoli spears into boiling water and cook for 7 or 8 minutes. Drain. Arrange broccoli spears in 2 12 × 20 × 4-inch pans. Dot each pan with 3 cups of margarine. Drizzle lemon juice over cooked broccoli. Serve immediately.

Candied Sweet Potatoes ½-cup servings

4 #10 cans cut sweet potatoes, drained
2 pounds brown sugar
1 tablespoon salt
2 tablespoons cinnamon
1 quart water

Place drained sweet potatoes in 2 12 × 20 × 4-inch pans. Combine other ingredients and pour over sweet potatoes in pans. Cook uncovered in oven at 375° for 30–45 minutes or until syrup is thick and potatoes are slightly browned and coated with syrup. Note: Potatoes may need to be basted with syrup to assure coating.

Buttered Minted Carrots ½-cup servings

4 #10 cans carrot coins
3 pounds margarine
2 pounds brown sugar
2 cups chopped fresh mint

Empty carrot coins into 2 12 × 20 × 4-inch pans. Dot with butter and brown sugar. Sprinkle chopped mint leaves over carrots. Cover pans and place in oven at 350° for 45 minutes.

Copper Pennies ½-cup servings

4 #10 cans carrots, sliced into coins
1 #10 can tomato soup, undiluted
6 large green peppers
6 large onions, sliced into rings
4 cups vinegar
3 cups sugar
3 cups vegetable oil
½ cup prepared mustard
½ cup Worcestershire sauce

Layer the first four ingredients in a 12 × 20 × 6-inch pan. Bring the remaining ingredients to a boil and pour over the carrots, onions and peppers. Cover and refrigerate for 12–24 hours before serving.

Corn on the Cob — 1 piece per serving

100 pieces corn on the cob (usually packed 96 per case)
4 gallons boiling water
½ cup salt
1 pound margarine

Boil water in 20-quart stock pot. Add salt. Drop corn into water and cover pot. Cook for 8–10 minutes. Drain. Transfer to serving pans and dot with margarine. Cover and allow margarine to melt. Individual pieces may be brushed with margarine before serving if desired. (Black pepper is an optional seasoning.)

Confetti Corn — ½-cup servings

4 #10 cans whole kernel corn
6 cups canned red and green peppers
1 pound margarine

Pour into 2 12 × 20 × 4-inch pans. Place in oven at 350° until corn is heated thoroughly. Serve immediately. Do not prepare ahead.

Corn Pudding — ½-cup servings

3 #10 cans cream style corn
24 eggs, beaten
6 cups sugar
1 pound margarine, melted
½ gallon reconstituted nonfat dry milk

Mix all ingredients in large container. Pour into 2 12 × 20 × 4-inch pans. Bake at 350° for 35–45 minutes or until pudding is set.

Green Peas in Potato Nest ½-cup servings

4 pounds instant potato granules or flakes
1¾ gallons boiling water
1 pound margarine
3 tablespoons salt
2½ quarts milk
10 pounds frozen green peas
½ pound margarine
2 tablespoons salt
Paprika for garnish

Prepare potatoes in mixer. A 20-quart mixer will prepare 100 servings in one batch, but if using a 12-quart mixer, ingredients will need to be halved and prepared in two batches. Pour water, margarine, and salt into mixer. Add potato granules or flakes gradually, thinning with milk as mixture thickens. Cook peas in small amount of water until tender. Drain. Season with margarine. Portion potatoes with a #16 scoop onto plates as served. Scoop peas into center of potato mound with solid spoon or #16 scoop. Total serving ½ cup.

Frozen Green Peas with Mushrooms ½-cup servings

20 pounds frozen green peas
1 #10 can small whole mushrooms
1 pound margarine
2 tablespoons ground nutmeg
2 tablespoons salt

Cook peas in stock pot or in 12 × 20 × 4-inch pans in oven at 350° as desired. Heat mushrooms in saucepan. Drain. Add to cooked peas and mix lightly. Season with salt and nutmeg. Serve immediately. Do not prepare ahead.

Hot Curried Fruit ½-cup servings

1 #10 can sliced apples
1 #10 can chunk pineapple
1 #10 can mixed fruit
1 #10 can sliced peaches
1 #303 can maraschino cherries, drained

Divide fruits, ½ can in each of 2 12 × 20 × 4-inch pans. Season each pan with 2 tablespoons curry powder. Dip out 2 cups fruit juice and mix with cornstarch. Return to pans, 1 cup into each. Cook uncovered at 350° for 45 minutes or until juice has thickened and flavors have mixed.

Hot Potato Salad 110 ½-cup servings

8 pounds instant potato granules or flakes
3½ gallons water, boiling
1½ pounds margarine
½ cup salt
1 cup sugar
1 gallon milk
24 hard cooked eggs, chopped
4 cups pickle relish

Mix water, margarine, and salt. Add granules or flakes, salt and sugar. Add milk. Mixture should be thick.

NOTE: See mixing instructions under recipe for Peas in Potato Nest. Blend in chopped eggs and pickle relish. Portion with a #8 scoop.

Southern Potato Salad ½-cup servings

20 pounds red potatoes, peeled and boiled, or
4 #10 cans tiny whole potatoes, drained and halved, or
4 pounds dehydrated diced potatoes, reconstituted
36 hard-cooked eggs
3 tablespoons salt (less if using canned potatoes)
1 stalk celery, chopped
2 large onions, chopped
1 quart sweet pickle relish
1½ quarts mayonnaise
2 pounds bacon, cooked crisp and crumbled

Mix all ingredients except bacon. Turn into serving pans and sprinkle bacon over top of potato salad. Serve with a large serving spoon in order to retain appearance of bacon.

Escalloped Potatoes ½-cup servings

5 pounds dehydrated sliced potatoes (reconstituted)
1 pound melted margarine
1 pound flour
2 gallons milk, heated
2 cups chopped onion
¼ cup salt
1 pound shredded cheese

Place reconstituted potatoes in two serving pans. Make a thin white sauce with the margarine, flour and milk. Spread onion over potatoes and cover with white sauce. Cover pans and cook at 350° for 45 minutes. Uncover and sprinkle cheese over potatoes. Reduce heat to 300° and continue cooking until potatoes are tender and cheese is melted.

Parslied Potatoes ½-cup servings

20 pounds red potatoes
2 pounds melted margarine
1 cup chopped dry parsley or 2 cups chopped fresh parsley

Scrub skins of potatoes and cut into chunks without peeling. Boil in salted water until potatoes are tender. Transfer to serving pans and drizzle with melted margarine. Add parsley and toss lightly. Add salt if desired.

Twice-Baked Potatoes ½ large potato

50 large white baking potatoes
Milk, margarine, and seasonings as desired
1 pound shredded cheese

Scrub and pierce potatoes with fork. Bake in oven at 350° until tender. Slice in half lengthwise and scoop out inside, leaving enough potato in each shell to hold its shape. Mash and season scooped-out potato as desired, adding milk to make mixture light and fluffy. Pile back into potato shells and bake at 350° until shells are slightly crisp and cheese is melted.

NOTE: Seasonings and milk cannot be accurately calculated for this recipe because of variation in size of potatoes and thickness of potato left in shell.

Seasoned Greens ½-cup servings

20 pounds frozen turnip, mustard, spinach, kale, or broccoli, or
25 pounds fresh greens

Cook greens in small amount of water, adding 4 tablespoons salt for 100 servings. Season with 1 pound margarine, 1½ cups vegetable oil, 4 cups chopped cooked ham, or 1 cup bacon drippings as desired. Cook only until tender. Do not overcook.

NOTE: 4 #10 cans greens may be used. Omit or reduce salt if using canned greens.

Vegetable Medley ½-cup servings

1 #10 can very young tender green peas
1 #10 can French style green beans
1 #10 can can white whole kernel corn (or yellow if preferred)
1 cup diced pimiento
1 quart celery, chopped fine
1 quart red onion, chopped fine
6 cups sugar
3 cups vinegar
3 cups oil

Pour ½ the liquid off each can of vegetables. Mix canned and raw vegetables. Combine vinegar, oil, and sugar and bring to a boil. Pour over mixed vegetables, in 2 serving pans. Cover and refrigerate for 12–24 hours.

NOTE: This keeps well in the refrigerator for several days.

Farm-Fresh Vegetables

Purchase seasonal vegetables according to amounts suggested in purchasing tables. Prepare according to regional traditions. Following are suggested combinations:

Lima Beans and Baby Carrots
Carrots, Onions, and Celery
Zucchini Squash and Tomatoes
Broccoli and Cauliflower
Green Peas and Pearl Onions
Corn and Lima Beans
Green Cabbage and Red Cabbage
Okra and Tomatoes

Hoppin' John — ¾-cup servings

6 #10 cans black-eyed peas
2 pounds bacon, cooked crisp (reserve fat)
6 medium onions
6 cloves garlic, minced
1 28-ounce box precooked rice
9 cups water
2 tablespoons salt
1 tablespoon chopped hot red pepper (optional)

Simmer the peas in a 20-quart stock pot for 15 minutes. Fry the bacon and set aside. Cook onion and garlic in bacon fat and add to the peas (including the fat). Prepare the rice with the 9 cups of water and season with salt. Transfer the peas to 2 12 × 20 × 4-inch pans. Add the rice and mix gently. Stir in pepper as desired. Garnish with crumbled bacon over the peas just before serving.

Yellow Squash Casserole — ½-cup servings

4 #10 cans sliced yellow squash
6 large onions
3 tablespoons salt
1 teaspoon pepper
1 pound margarine
1 cup sugar
12 eggs, beaten
1 pound sharp cheese, shredded

Drain squash. Cook onions in squash liquid until crisp and tender. Mash squash and season with salt, pepper, margarine, and sugar. Add onion and beaten eggs and mix well. Fold in cheese. Pour into 2 well-greased 12 × 20-inch pans. Bake in oven at 325° until mixture has set.

Williamsburg Ratatouille — ½-cup servings

12 medium zucchini squash, sliced
1 stalk celery
6 large onions
6 large green peppers
2 medium egg plants
2 #10 cans whole tomatoes (drain ½ juice and reserve)
3 tablespoons garlic powder
3 tablespoons oregano
3 tablespoons basil
3 tablespoons salt
1 tablespoon black pepper
2 cups Parmesan cheese

Slice fresh vegetables and divide between 2 12 × 20 × 4-inch pans. Add 1 can tomatoes to each pan and add mixed seasonings. Cover pans and bake in oven at 350° for 45 minutes. Uncover and sprinkle each pan with 1 cup Parmesan cheese. Return to oven and bake 15 additional minutes (uncovered) or until vegetables are tender. Add some reserved tomato juice if vegetables become dry.

Escalloped Tomatoes — ½-cup servings

4 #10 cans tomatoes
1 cup sugar
1 cup margarine
1 teaspoon black pepper
4 quarts bread crumbs

Heat first four ingredients together, then pour into 2 12 × 20 × 4-inch pans. Add ½ the bread crumbs. Stir lightly, mixing crumbs into tomatoes. Top with remaining crumbs and bake in oven at 350° for 20 minutes or until crumb topping is browned and tomatoes are thick.

SALADS

Broccoli Salad — ½-cup servings

10 pounds fresh broccoli, cut into bite-size pieces
2 medium heads lettuce, shredded
3 pounds red onion rings
5 pounds halved cherry tomatoes or tomato wedges

Mix broccoli, lettuce, and onion rings. Add tomatoes gently. Toss lightly with Italian dressing.

Chef's Salad — ¾-cup servings

8 medium heads lettuce, broken into bite-size pieces
1 pound spinach leaves
2 pounds red radishes, sliced
3 pounds carrots, sliced crosswise
1 medium head red cabbage, shredded

Wash and chill vegetables. Cut as designated. Mix vegetables lightly and serve with choice of dressings. Tomato wedges make an attractive garnish for serving container or for each salad serving.

Chef's Salad Version 2 — ¾-cup servings

8 heads lettuce
5 pounds tomatoes, cubed
5 pounds cucumbers, sliced thin
3 pounds shredded carrots
1 medium head red cabbage
6 large green peppers, chopped

Mix as directed above, tossing lightly. Serve with choice of dressing.

Basic Slaw — ½-cup servings

15 pounds cabbage, shredded
2 pounds celery, finely chopped
2 pounds onion, finely chopped
4 pounds carrots, finely chopped
1 head red cabbage, finely shredded
2 tablespoons salt
2½ quarts salad dressing or mayonnaise

Shred or chop cabbage in food processor, being careful not to over process. Chop other vegetables and mix with cabbage. Season with salt. Mix lightly with dressing. Serve at once. Do not prepare ahead.

VARIATION: Vinegar Slaw—Instead of mayonnaise, use dressing made from 3 cups vinegar, 3 cups salad oil, 3 cups sugar and 3 tablespoons celery seed.

Cherry Congealed Salad — 2-inch squares

1 24-ounce package cherry gelatin
1 #10 can crushed pineapple (drained juice reserved)
1 #10 can sweet bing cherries (drained juice reserved)
Water
1 2-liter cola drink
1 pound cream cheese, softened
1 64-ounce can pecans, chopped

Heat drained fruit juice to boiling. Dissolve gelatin in boiling juice. Add water if necessary to measure 2 quarts. Chill until syrupy, then add cola and let stand until thickened. Add softened cream cheese and nuts, mixing until smooth. Pour into 2 12 × 20 × 2-inch pans and allow to congeal. Serve on a lettuce leaf garnished with a dollop of mayonnaise.

English Pea Salad — ½-cup servings

4 #10 cans young tender English Peas
24 hard-cooked eggs, chopped
1 quart pickle relish
1 pound American cheese, shredded
2 quarts mayonnaise

Mix all ingredients except cheese. Spread shredded cheese on top of salad. Serve with a spoon to retain appearance.

Frozen Fruit Salad — 2½-inch portions

1 #10 can mandarin orange sections
1 #10 can pineapple chunks
1 #10 can sliced peaches
2 pounds miniature marshmallows
2 quarts dairy sour cream
100 lettuce leaves

Drain canned fruits. Combine all ingredients and pour into 2 12 × 20 × 2-inch pans. Freeze. Cut 48 servings from each pan. Serve on a lettuce leaf garnished with a maraschino cherry.

Pickled Beets with Onion Rings — ¼-cup servings

2 #10 cans sliced beets
2 quarts vinegar
4 cups sugar
¼ cup ground cloves
6 large onions, sliced into rings

Drain beets. Heat vinegar, sugar, and cloves to boiling and pour over beets. Cover and chill for 24 hours, stirring occasionally to mix flavors. Slice onion rings over beets. Serve one onion ring with each 3 or 4 slices of beets.

Rosy Pear Salad — 1 pear half per serving

3 #10 cans pear halves, drained
2 6-ounce packages cream cheese, whipped
1 32-ounce jar marshmallow cream
1 family-size package red gelatin (any flavor)
100 lettuce leaves

Mix whipped cream cheese with marshmallow cream. Place each pear half on a lettuce leaf. Spoon about 2 teaspoons cream cheese mixture into the cavity of each pear. Sprinkle with ¼ teaspoon dry red gelatin powder.

NOTE: 1 #10 can usually yields 30–35 pear halves, depending on the brand. Check the count on the can or buy an extra can for safety.

Stuffed Peach Halves — 1 peach half per serving

3 #10 cans peach halves
1 quart whole cranberry sauce
1 quart peanut butter
1 tablespoon ground cloves
100 lettuce leaves

Mix peanut butter, cranberry sauce, and cloves. Portion into peach halves with a #40 scoop. Serve on a lettuce leaf garnished with a mint sprig or a parsley sprig.

NOTE: Check count on cans. One #10 can usually contains 30–35 peach halves, depending upon the brand purchased.

Layered Vegetable Salad

4 medium heads lettuce
4 1-pound bags frozen green peas, thawed, not cooked
2 pounds shredded cheese
6 cups cooked rice, cooled
12 hard-cooked eggs
4 large red onions, sliced into rings
1 stalk celery, chopped, including leaves
2 16-ounce cans chopped pimiento

Layer as listed above in 2 12 × 20 × 4-inch pans beginning and ending with lettuce.

Dressing

2 quarts mayonnaise
2 quarts buttermilk
2 cups chopped parsley
¼ cup garlic powder
¼ cup onion powder

Drizzle over salad just before serving.

BREADS

Basic Yeast Dough for Rolls — 2-inch rolls

1½ quarts milk
1 cup sugar
½ cup dry yeast
2 tablespoons salt
5 quarts plain flour
1½ cups melted vegetable shortening

Scald milk, then cool to lukewarm. Pour into mixer bowl. Add sugar and yeast and allow to stand for 5 minutes. Mix salt with flour. Add ½ the flour and the melted shortening to the milk mixture. Mix well. Add the remaining flour and mix with dough hook until dough sticks together and leaves the sides of the bowl. Cover and allow to rise until double its bulk. Punch down and knead on lightly floured surface until dough is elastic and well mixed. Roll to ¾-inch thickness and cut out rolls. Place on lightly greased 18 × 26-inch baking pan. (1 pan will hold 108 2-in. rolls.) Allow to rise in a warm place. Bake in oven at 400° until light brown. Brush with margarine if desired.

VARIATIONS:

WHEAT ROLLS—Replace half the flour with wheat flour. Mix and bake as above.

CINNAMON ROLLS—Mix basic roll dough. Work with ½ the dough at a time. Roll into a long rectangle, ¼-inch thick and about 12 inches wide. Spread dough with melted margarine, sugar, and cinnamon. Roll, jelly-roll style, and cut into ¾-inch slices. Place on well-greased pans and allow to rise. Bake in oven at 350° until lightly brown. For icing, use 3 cups confectioners sugar and enough milk and vanilla flavoring to make thick syrup. Drizzle over rolls.

CRESCENT ROLLS—Roll dough ⅜-inch thick. Cut into 3-inch squares. Cut each square into triangles. Brush with margarine and roll each triangle, beginning with flat side and ending with point on top. Place on baking pans and bend into crescent shape. Allow to rise and bake the same as rolls.

POCKET ROLLS—Roll to ⅜-inch thickness. Cut with large cutter. Brush with margarine and fold each roll in half. Allow to rise and bake like basic rolls.

CLOVER LEAF ROLLS—Grease 100 muffin tins. Roll dough into balls the size to fit three into muffin tins. Allow to rise. Bake as above.

LOAF BREAD—Mix as for rolls. Divide dough into three portions. Place into 2 pound-loaf pans and allow to rise. Bake in oven at 400° for 30–35 minutes.

TEXAS TOAST—Prepare loaves of bread as described above. Allow loaves to season for 24 hours. Slice thick and spread with margarine. Toast and serve hot.

GARLIC TOAST—Prepare as above. Sprinkle with garlic salt after toast is spread with margarine. (Garlic and parsley salt adds a bit of color as well as flavor.)

Biscuits — 2-inch biscuits

4 pounds self-rising flour
3½ cups solid vegetable shortening
1 quart milk

Cut shortening into flour. Add milk and mix until dough sticks together and leaves edges of bowl. Divide dough into halves and knead each portion for about 5 minutes on a lightly floured surface. Roll to ½-inch thickness and cut with a 2-inch cutter. Place on an 18 × 26-inch baking pan. (Note: one pan will hold 108 biscuits.) Bake in oven at 425° for 12–15 minutes.

VARIATIONS:

YEAST BISCUITS—Dissolve ¼ cup yeast in 1 cup warm water. Reduce quantity of milk by 1 cup, adding yeast mixture. Mix and bake as above. (No proofing time necessary.)

CHEESE BISCUITS—Add 4 cups shredded cheese to flour. Mix and bake as above.

Mexican Corn Bread

Corn-bread recipe appears with recipe for Creamed Turkey (p. 48).

MEXICAN VARIATION: Add ½ #10 can yellow cream style corn, 1 pound shredded cheese, and 2 cups chopped green chili peppers to basic corn-bread recipe. Bake as directed.

Monkey Bread

10 cans biscuits
1 pound margarine, melted
½ cup cinnamon
2 cups sugar
5 tube pans or bundt cake pans, greased generously

Mix cinnamon and sugar. Dip biscuits in melted margarine then in cinnamon sugar. Stack in cake pans until pans are ⅔ filled. Bake in oven at 375° for 20 minutes or until top is golden brown. Turn out onto serving plates. Biscuits will pull apart.

DESSERTS

Ambrosia — ½-cup servings

2 #10 cans mandarin orange sections
2 #10 cans pineapple chunks
3 quarts shredded coconut
2 pounds miniature marshmallows

Drain fruits and mix with coconut. Stir marshmallows until they begin to melt. Mix well and fold this mixture into the fruit-coconut mixture. Chill.

Banana Pudding — ½-cup servings

2 cups instant vanilla pudding mix
3 quarts milk
1 64-ounce can sweetened condensed milk
2 16-ounce cartons whipped topping
3 pounds vanilla wafers
24 bananas

Empty instant pudding mix into large bowl, add milk. Add condensed milk and whipped topping and mix with a wire whip. Layer vanilla wafers and bananas in 2 12 × 20 × 2-inch pans. Cover with pudding mixture. Repeat. Garnish with vanilla wafer crumbs if desired.

Quick Fruit Cobbler ½-cup servings

2 pounds margarine
2 quarts plain flour
2 quarts sugar
1½ quarts milk
2 #10 cans fruit (including juice)

Melt the margarine (1 lb. in each of 2 12 × 20 × 2-inch pans). Mix a thin batter with the flour, sugar, and milk. Pour batter over margarine in pans. Add 1 can of fruit and juice. Bake in oven at 350° for 40 minutes or until crust has risen to top of pan and is golden brown.

NOTE: Peaches, apples, blueberries, mixed fruit, or sweetened cherries are good choices for this dessert. Prepared fruit pie fillings may also be used, but use only half the sugar in the recipe above.

Fruit Cobbler Version 2 ½-cup servings

2 #10 cans fruit and juice
1 5-pound box prepared biscuit mix
5 cups cold water

Pour fruit into 2 12 × 20 × 2-inch pans. Heat in hot oven until bubbly. Prepare thick batter from biscuit mix and water. Drop by tablespoons onto fruit in pans. Bake at 425° until biscuits are golden brown.

Fruit Crisp ½-cup servings

2 #10 cans apples, peaches, or other canned fruit
1 4½-pound box yellow cake mix
1 pound margarine melted

Pour 1 #10 can of fruit into each of 2 12 × 20 × 2-inch pans. Spread the cake mix over the fruit. Bake in oven at 350° for 30 minutes or until cake mix is crisp and fruit is bubbly.

Fruit Gelatin — ½-cup servings

3 pounds fruit flavored gelatin
2 gallons boiling water
2 #10 cans fruit cocktail
12 ripe bananas, sliced

Mix gelatin and boiling water. Refrigerate until mixture thickens. Add fruit and allow to set. Cut in squares or spoon into sherbet dishes.

Chocolate Ice-Box Pie — 96 2 × 2½-inch servings

3 quarts graham cracker crumbs
1 pound melted margarine
2 #10 cans ready-to-eat chocolate pudding
64 ounces prepared whipped topping
1 pound finely chopped nuts

Mix the graham cracker crumbs and the margarine in 2 12 × 20 × 2-inch pans. Refrigerate and allow to set. Spread one can chocolate pudding in each pan and top each with 32 ounces whipped topping and ½ pound nuts. Serve very cold.

Chocolate Brownies

2 6-pound boxes brownie mix

Prepare according to package directions. Bake on 2 18 × 26-inch baking pans and cut into 3-inch squares. Top with a scoop of ice cream for a rich dessert.

Peach Delight

2 #10 cans peach slices, drained
3 10-ounce packages miniature marshmallows
2 16-ounce cartons whipped topping
1 12-ounce package vanilla wafers, crushed

Mix peach slices with marshmallows in 2 12 × 20 × 2-inch pans. Fold in whipped topping. Sprinkle crumbs on top. Serve chilled.

Pound Cake — 90 1-inch slices

2 5-pound boxes pound cake mix
18 eggs
Water and oil as directed on box

Mix according to package directions. Bake in 10 9-inch loaf pans. Cool in pan. Cut in 1-inch slices.

NOTE: Number of eggs may vary according to brand of cake mix. The number given above is the usual number of eggs required and is included as a help for purchasing supplies.

Iced Cake Squares — 96 3-inch squares

2 4½-pound boxes yellow cake mix
18 eggs
2 cups vegetable oil
2½ quarts water
2 4-pound boxes frosting mix

Mix according to package directions. Bake on 2 18 × 26-inch baking sheets. Spread with frosting. Cut into 3-inch squares. Each pan makes 48.

VARIATION: Strawberry Shortcake—Bake sheet cake according to above directions. Top each square with ¼ cup fresh or frozen strawberries. Garnish with whipped topping if desired.

NOTE: Number of eggs may vary with brand of cake mix. Number of eggs above is given as a help in purchasing supplies.

Bread Pudding

24 eggs
1 quart sugar
2 tablespoons salt
½ cup vanilla
½ cup margarine
1½ gallons hot milk
9 quarts dry bread crumbs
2 quarts raisins

Beat eggs, sugar, salt, and vanilla together. Add hot milk and margarine to this mixture. Spread bread crumbs and raisins in 2 12 × 20 × 4-inch pans. Pour custard mixture over bread and raisins, making sure bread crumbs are well saturated. Bake in slow oven at 325° for 40 minutes or until set. Serve warm using a #12 scoop.

VARIATIONS:

RICE PUDDING—Substitute 2 gallons cooked rice for the bread crumbs. Mix and bake as directed above.

CHOCOLATE BREAD PUDDING: Substitute 10 melted chocolate mint patties per pan for raisins. Mix and bake as directed above. When serving bread pudding, the following topping makes a delicious addition.

Hard Sauce: for 100 servings
2½ pounds margarine
7½ cups powdered sugar
7½ teaspoons vanilla

Cream margarine till very soft. Stir in sugar and vanilla. Whip till smooth and creamy. Serve on the side of the pudding using a #24 scoop.

Prune Squares — 108 2-inch squares

2½ quarts flour
2 quarts sugar
2 tablespoons salt
2 quarts rolled oats
2½ pounds melted margarine
6 quarts prunes, cooked and chopped
3 tablespoons cinnamon

Combine the first 5 ingredients and press half of mixture into an 18 × 26-inch pan. Spread prunes over crust and sprinkle with cinnamon. Top with remainder of crust mixture. Bake in oven at 350° for 30 minutes or until crust is lightly browned and crisp. Cut into 2-inch squares. Serve warm with a dollop of whipped topping.

Cookie Recipes

NOTE: Although cookie dough is avilable in many varieties and flavors, there is something special about homemade cookies. For that reason, two favorite cookie recipes are included below.

Tea Cakes — 2-inch cakes

3½ cups sugar
1 pound margarine
6 eggs
2½ quarts plain flour
¼ cup baking powder
2 teaspoons salt
1½ teaspoons nutmeg
2 tablespoons vanilla
1½ cups milk

Cream margarine and sugar. Add eggs and mix well. Mix dry ingredients and add alternately with milk. Portion with a #40 scoop onto greased baking sheets. Bake in oven at 400° for 8–10 minutes.

Oatmeal Cookies — 2½-inch cookies

2 quarts plain flour
1 tablespoon soda
1 tablespoon salt
1 tablespoon cinnamon
1 tablespoon nutmeg
2 pounds margarine
4 cups brown sugar
2 cups white sugar
1 cup buttermilk
4 cups raisins
1 gallon rolled oats
8 eggs

Mix flour, soda, salt, and spices. Soak raisins in buttermilk while mixing other ingredients. Cream margarine and sugars. Add eggs. Add flour mixture and mix lightly. Stir in oats, raisins and buttermilk. Portion with a #30 scoop and bake in oven at 375° for 8–10 minutes.

NOTE: If chewy cookies are desired, bake until just set and lightly browned. If allowed to become darker brown, cookies will be crisp.

Chess Pie — 104 servings

13 9-inch pie shells
36 eggs
3 quarts sugar
¼ cup vanilla
1 cup corn meal
½ cup vinegar
2 pounds margarine, melted

Beat eggs, sugar, and vanilla in mixer bowl. Add cornmeal, vinegar, and melted margarine. Mix thoroughly on low speed. Pour into pie shells (about 2 cups per shell). Bake in oven at 350° for 30–40 minutes. Cut each pie into 8 servings.

Chocolate Cake — 100 3×4-inch servings

2¾ quarts self-rising flour
2½ quarts sugar
3 cups cocoa
2 tablespoons baking soda
3½ cups softened vegetable shortening
14 eggs
2 tablespoons vanilla
1¾ quarts milk

Blend dry ingredients in mixer on low speed. Add shortening, eggs, vanilla, and half the milk, blending for 5 minutes on low speed. Beat 2 minutes on medium speed. Add remaining milk and beat two more minutes on medium speed. Pour into 2 18×26-inch, well-greased pans, using about 1 gallon batter per pan. Bake in oven at 350° for 35 minutes or until cake springs back from touch and begins to loosen from edges of pan.

Chocolate Icing

6 pounds powdered sugar
2 cups softened vegetable shortening
2 cups cocoa
Milk as necessary for desired consistency

VARIATION: Black Forest Cake—Bake cake as directed above and frost as follows: Combine 1 #10 can cherry pie filling with 1 tablespoon almond extract. Sporead over cake. Spread 12 cups whipped topping over pie filling. Sprinkle 2 cups toasted slivered almonds over whipped topping. Cut into portions and serve as above.

Rainbow Cake

1 4½-pound box white cake mix
Water and egg whites as directed on package

Bake white cake mix as directed. While cake is baking, prepare 2 6-ounce packages cherry or strawberry gelatin using all hot water. While cake is hot, punch holes randomly in cake and pour liquid gelatin over cake, allowing it to run into holes in cake. Refrigerate, allowing gelatin to set.

Sugar Plum Pudding — 100 2 × 2½-inch servings

3¾ cups vegetable shortening
1¾ quarts sugar
10 eggs
2 tablespoons soda
2½ quarts flour
3 tablespoons cinnamon
2 tablespoons nutmeg
1¼ quarts buttermilk
1¼ quarts cooked prunes, chopped

Cream sugar and shortening. Add eggs and mix thoroughly. Mix dry ingredients and add alternately with buttermilk. Fold in prunes and mix lightly. Bake in well-greased 18 × 26-inch pan for 35–45 minutes or until firm. Remove from oven and pour glaze over cake while it is warm.

Glaze

2½ cups margarine
2½ cups buttermilk
1¼ quarts sugar
2 tablespoons vanilla

Combine first 3 ingredients and bring to a boil. Remove and add vanilla. Pour over warm cake above.

Red Velvet Cake — 96 servings

2 cups red food color
1½ cups cocoa
4 cups shortening
12 cups sugar
16 eggs
4½ quarts flour
4 teaspoons salt
2 quarts. buttermilk
5 tablespoons vanilla
5 tablespoons almond extract
1 cup vinegar
3 tablespoons soda

Mix cocoa and food coloring. Cream together with shortening, sugar, and eggs. Add salt to flour and add this mixture alternately with buttermilk. Blend in flavorings. Mix vinegar and soda and add to other mixture quickly. Mix well. Bake in 2 12×20×2-inch baking pans. Frost with white frosting. Each pan yields 48 2×2½ inch servings.

Sweet Potato Pie — 104 servings

13 unbaked pie shells (deep dish)
2 #10 cans solid pack sweet potatoes
1½ cups margarine
1 gallon milk
3 pounds brown sugar
24 eggs
⅓ cup pumpkin pie spice

Mix all ingredients in mixer. Pour into pie shells, allowing about 4 cups per shell. Bake in oven at 375° for 50 minutes or until filling is set and pastry is golden brown. Serve warm or cooled with a dollop of whipped topping.

Menus for Women's Luncheons

Curried Ham Rolls
Frozen Fruit Salad on Lettuce
Cheese Rolls
Carrot Cake

Hot Chicken Salad
Dark Cherry Squares on Lettuce
Raisin Bran Muffins
Caramel Sundae

Fresh Fruit Salad with Cottage Cheese
and Custard Dressing
Cream Cheese Sandwiches on Nut Bread
Orange Danish

Cornish Hens with Orange Sauce
Wild Rice
Mixed Pickled Vegetables
Strawberry Pretzel Salad
Hot Biscuits
Petit Fours

Turkey Divine
Sweet Potatoes in Orange Half
Clover Leaf Rolls
Butterscotch Nut Squares

Chicken Mousse
Waldorf Salad
Whole Wheat Rolls
Orange Sherbet

Quiche Lorraine
Marinated Asparagus Spears   Tomato Aspic
Herbed Toast Points
Strawberry Parfait

Shrimp Macaroni Salad on Lettuce
Stuffed Celery Hearts   Fruit Compote
Tiny Hot Rolls
Ice Cream Sandwiches

Broccoli and Cheese Soup
Egg Salad in Pita Bread
Crunchy Vegetables and Dip
Chocolate-Dipped Strawberries

Cream of Corn Soup
Dainty Cucumber Sandwiches
Peppermint Party Salad
Orange Danish Rolls

French Onion Soup
Open-Faced Toasted Cheese Sandwiches
Fresh Grapefruit Salad
Grasshopper Tarts

Gourmet Potato Soup
Vegetable Lasagna
Toast Rounds
Cheese Cake

Chicken Salad in Fresh Pineapple Quarters
Chilled Red Grapes
Bran Muffins
French Vanilla Ice-Cream Balls

California Pasta Salad
Assorted Cheese and Crackers
Cherry Tarts

Curried Tuna Salad in Lettuce Cup
Fresh Melon and Avocado Slices
Cheese and Crackers
Lemon Pie

Recipes for Women's Luncheons—Fifty Servings

MAIN DISHES

Curried Ham Rolls

4 quarts cooked rice
2 cups chopped onion
2 cups chopped fresh parsley
½ cup margarine
1 tablespoon salt
1 tablespoon curry powder
50 slices boiled ham

Mix first 6 ingredients. Portion ⅓ cup rice mixture onto each slice of ham. Roll and place in 12 × 20 inch pan seam side down. Pour curry sauce over ham rolls and bake in oven at 350° for 30 minutes. Spoon 1 tablespoon sauce over each roll and garnish with a sprig of parsley. Serve on toast points if desired.

Curry Sauce

1 cup margarine
1 tablespoon curry powder
1 tablespoon monosodium glutenate
½ cup cornstarch

1 tablespoon salt
3 quarts milk

Melt margarine. Add curry, monosodium glutenate, cornstarch, and salt. Blend well. Add milk. Cook over low heat until mixture thickens. Do not boil.

Hot Chicken Salad

20 chicken breasts, cooked, skinned, deboned and chopped
6 cups chopped celery
1 tablespoon salt
1 tablespoon monosodium glutenate
2 cups minced onion
3 cups slivered almonds
1 cup lemon juice
1 quart mayonnaise
3 6-ounce cans water chestnuts, thinly sliced
1 16-ounce package potato chips, crushed
4 cups shredded cheddar cheese

Mix together first 9 ingredients in a 12 × 20-inch baking pan. Top with shredded cheese and potato chips. Bake in oven at 450° for 15 minutes or until chips are brown and cheese is melted.

NOTE: Onion and celery remain crunchy.

Cornish Hens with Orange Sauce on Wild Rice

25 cornish hens, halved
12 cloves garlic
3 cups lemon juice

Mix lemon juice and minced garlic. Marinate hens overnight in lemon mixture. Place hens on rack in oven at 400° and bake for 45 minutes to 1 hour or until browned and tender. Place each half on a bed of wild rice and spoon orange sauce over hens and rice.

Wild Rice

5 pounds dry wild rice or long grain and wild rice mixed.

Prepare according to packer's directions.

Orange Sauce

3 cups sugar
1 tablespoon salt
½ cup cornstarch
3 cups orange juice
2 tablespoons grated orange peel

Mix salt, sugar, and cornstarch. Stir in orange juice and cook over medium heat until mixture thickens and boils. Remove from heat and stir in grated orange peel. Cool to lukewarm and spoon over Cornish hens.

Turkey Divine

50 3-ounce slices cooked turkey breast (9 lbs. cooked)
100 broccoli spears cooked crisp tender
1 #10 can prepared cheese sauce
1 cup chopped parsley

Place hot cooked broccoli spears in baking pans, 2 spears together, floweretts facing opposite directions. Cover each 2 spears with a slice of cooked turkey breast. Cover and heat until turkey slices are hot. Heat the cheese sauce and spoon over turkey as served. Sprinkle with parsley.

Chicken Mousse

10 cups finely diced cooked chicken
2 cups chopped olives
2 cups chopped celery
1 cup chopped pimiento
1 cup chopped pecans
1 ounce unflavored gelatin
4 cups hot chicken stock
2 cups mayonnaise
1 cup evaporated milk

Combine first 5 ingredients. Dissolve gelatin in chicken stock. Add mayonnaise and evaporated milk. Combine this mixture with chicken mixture and stir until mixed. Pour into 4 12-inch loaf pans. Chill until firm. For ease in unmolding, dip pan in hot water. Slice into 1-inch slices. Garnish each slice with a green pepper ring and a dab of mayonnaise.

Quiche Lorraine — 49 servings

7 deep-dish pie shells
3½ cups chopped onion
3½ cups chopped celery
1 cup margarine
2½ pounds shredded mozzarella cheese
2½ pounds American processed cheese
3½ cups bacon cooked and crumbled
24 eggs well beaten
1 tablespoon salt
1 gallon milk

Cook the onion and celery in the margarine over low heat until tender. Portion the cheeses and bacon into the pie shells. Add the onion and celery. Mix eggs, salt and milk and pour over other ingredients in pie shells. Bake in oven at 375° for 30 minutes. Cut each into 7 pieces. Serve warm, not hot.

Shrimp Macaroni Salad

3 8-ounce packages small shell macaroni (12 c. cooked)
6 cups cooked chopped shrimp
4 pounds frozen green peas (thawed, not cooked)
8 hard-cooked eggs, chopped
4 medium green peppers, chopped
1 cup stuffed olives, chopped
1 6-ounce can pimiento, chopped
1 large onion, chopped
1 tablespoon salt
1 quart mayonnaise

Mix all ingredients and chill. Serve with a #6 scoop onto a lettuce leaf.

Chicken Salad

3 quarts cooked cubed chicken
1 small minced onion
3 cups chopped celery
2 cups slivered almonds (toasted)
12 hard-cooked eggs, chopped
3 cups mayonnaise
1 cup lemon juice
1 tablespoon salt
1 teaspoon freshly ground black pepper
2 cups halved white seedless grapes
2 cups chopped fresh pineapple

Mix all ingredients except fruits. Add fruits and mix lightly. Chill and serve in pineapple shells.

Egg Salad — 50 servings in pita bread

60 hard-cooked eggs
2 quarts pickle relish, drained
1 quart mayonnaise
Pickle juice as desired

Mix all ingredients, adding pickle juice to achieve desired consistency.

Curried Tuna Salad

1 64-ounce can solid water-packed white tuna
12 green onions, chopped
6 medium red apples, chopped (unpeeled)
2 cups white raisins
3 cups finely chopped celery
16 hard-cooked eggs, chopped
3 tablespoons curry powder
¼ cup lemon juice
1 quart mayonnaise

Mix all ingredients and serve on lettuce leaves. Garnish with a thin slice of lemon twisted to form a bow effect.

California Pasta Salad

3 pounds corkscrew macaroni, cooked and drained
1 pound carrots, thinly sliced
1 pound green onions, chopped
1 16-ounce can pimiento, drained and chopped
3 16-ounce cans red kidney beans, drained
6 cups chopped celery
1 4-pound package frozen green peas, uncooked

1 cup chopped parsley
4 cups low calorie Italian dressing
50 lettuce leaves washed and chilled
13 medium tomatoes, sliced into 8 wedges
25 hard-cooked eggs, quartered
50 parsley sprigs for garnish

Mix first 9 ingredients, tossing until well mixed. Chill. Portion onto plates with #8 scoop. Garnish each serving with 2 tomato wedges, 2 egg wedges, and a sprig of parsley.

NOTE: Italian dressing may be purchased prepared or reconstituted from a dry mix. If a sweeter dressing is preferred, add dry artificial sweetener as desired.

Fresh Fruit Salad with Cottage Cheese and Custard Dressing

Arrange fresh fruits on individual serving plates as desired. Include seasonal favorites such as melon and peaches. Try some unusual fruits such as kiwi. Fresh pineapple and bananas are flavor staples for a fruit plate. Center each plate with a scoop of cottage cheese. Spoon custard dressing generously over fruits and cheese. Garnish with a stemmed maraschino cherry, either red or green.

Custard Dressing

2 6-ounce packages instant vanilla pudding mix
1 16-ounce can sweetened condensed milk
1 8-ounce carton whipped topping
1 tablespoon vanilla

Mix pudding according to package directions, using twice the amount of milk. Add other ingredients and allow to thicken.

Broccoli and Cheese Soup — 1-cup servings

4 cups chopped onion
1 cup margarine
1 #10 can cream of celery soup
1 #10 can can potato soup
2 quarts whole milk
2 quarts unsalted chicken broth (may be purchased canned if necessary)
4 pounds chopped broccoli, cooked crisp tender
2 pounds soft processed cheese, chopped into chunks

Cook onion in margarine over low heat until onion is tender. Add onion to soups which have been mixed. Blend in other liquids. Add chopped broccoli and simmer until mixture is heated. Do not boil. Add chunks of cheese 10 minutes before serving time. Cheese should be partly melted but visible in the soup bowls. Serve with a #8 ladle (1 cup).

Cream of Corn Soup — 1-cup servings

1 #10 can cream style corn
1 #10 can whole kernel corn
3 quarts whole milk
1 pint half-and-half
1 stick margarine
1 large onion, chopped
1 cup chopped parsley
1 tablespoon salt
1 teaspoon white pepper

Mix corn, milk, and half-and-half and simmer over low heat for 30 minutes. Cook onion in margarine until tender and add to corn mixture. Add parsley and seasonings and keep warm until serving time. Do not boil. Serve with a #8 ladle.

French Onion Soup — ¾-cup servings

1 pound margarine
12 large yellow onions, chopped
12 large white onions, sliced into rings
6 cloves garlic, finely chopped
1 cup flour
½ cup Worcestershire sauce
2 #10 cans beef consomme

Cook onions and garlic in margarine on low heat for 15 minutes. Add flour and stir. Cook 5 more minutes. Add consomme and Worcestershire sauce. Serve with a #6 ladle.

NOTE: Because of the strong flavor of onion soup, servings are smaller.

Gourmet Potato Soup — 1-cup servings

5 pounds white potatoes, peeled, diced and
  cooked in 1 gallon water and 2 tablespoons salt
6 large onions, diced and cooked with potatoes
1 gallon whole milk
3 cups chopped parsley
6 cups cooked ham, finely chopped or ground
1 pound shredded cheddar cheese

Remove cooked potatoes from water and process in food processor until partially but not totally pureed. Add pureed potatoes back to cooking water. Add milk and heat but do not boil. Just before serving time, add ham, cheese, and parsley and reheat. Serve with a #8 ladle.

NOTE: If soup is not thick enough, add 1 cup or more instant potato flakes to reach thickness desired.

FRUITS AND VEGETABLES

Dark Cherry Salad — 60 2-inch squares

3 6-ounce packages black cherry gelatin
3 cups boiling water
3 cups cold water
4 16-ounce cans dark sweet cherries, undrained
2 16-ounce cans crushed pineapple, undrained
1 20-ounce bag miniature marshmallows
2 cups chopped pecans
12 large bananas, chopped

Dissolve gelatin in boiling water. Add cold water. Stir in marshmallows. (Marshmallows should soften but not melt.) Add pineapple and cherries and pour into a 12 × 20-inch pan. Allow to chill until it thickens. Stir and add pecans and bananas. Return to refrigerator. Stir several times during setting time to keep well mixed.

Frozen Fruit Salad — 60 2-inch squares

2 29-ounce cans sliced peaches, undrained
2 29-ounce cans pears, chopped (save juice)
6 large bananas, sliced
2 10-ounce cans sweetened condensed milk
1 16-ounce carton whipped topping
1 10-ounce jar maraschino cherries, drained
2 cups chopped pecans

Mix all ingredients in a 12 × 20-inch pan. Freeze. Cut in squares. Serve on a lettuce leaf garnished with a stemmed maraschino cherry.

Strawberry Pretzel Salad — 60 2-inch squares

1 10-ounce box thin pretzels
4 sticks margarine
5 6-ounce packages cream cheese
3 cups sugar
2 10-ounce cartons whipped topping
2 6-ounce packages strawberry gelatin
4 cups boiling water
4 10-ounce packages frozen strawberries

Crush pretzels into small pieces, but not into crumbs. Spread in a 12 × 20-inch pan. Add melted margarine and mix well. Bake for 10 minutes in oven at 350°. Cool. Mix cream cheese, sugar, and 1 carton whipped topping. Spread over cooled pretzels. Refrigerate until set. Dissolve gelatin in water. Add strawberries (do not defrost). When this mixture thickens, add second carton whipped topping and mix. Pour over layers in the pan and allow to set.

Waldorf Salad

24 medium red apples, chopped, not peeled
1 medium stalk celery, chopped
6 cups chopped walnuts
1 10-ounce package miniature marshmallows
2 16-ounce packages raisins
1 quart mayonnaise

Mix all ingredients. Chill and serve with a #6 scoop

Frozen Peppermint Salad

3 29-ounce cans crushed pineapple
2 6-ounce packages cherry flavored gelatin
2 10-ounce packages miniature marshmallows
1 8-ounce package cinnamon red hot candies
1 pound butter mint candies
1 16-ounce carton whipped topping

Mix pineapple, dry gelatin, marshmallows, and cinnamon candies and allow to stand overnight at room temperature. Soften the butter mints in a saucepan and add to pineapple mixture. Fold in whipped topping and freeze until firm.

Fresh Grapefruit Salad

25 fresh grapefruits
1 quart cucumber dressing
6 small red onions
3 large heads lettuce

Allow ½ grapefruit for each serving, or purchase canned grapefruit sections and drain (8 29-ounce cans or 2 #10 cans). Arrange sections on a bed of shredded lettuce and use 1 tablespoon prepared cucumber dressing for each salad. Garnish with one red onion ring.

Hot Fruit Mixture

1 #10 can pear halves
1 #10 can pineapple chunks
1 #10 can red plums
4 cups light brown sugar
1 pound margarine
2 cups chopped pecans
1 tablespoon nutmeg and 1 tablespoon cinnamon (optional)

Drain cans of fruit. Layer fruits in a 12 × 20-inch pan as follows: pears, plums, pineapple. Mix sugar, margarine, nuts and spices (if desired). Spoon this mixture over fruits. Bake in oven at 350° for 45 minutes.

Marinated Asparagus Spears

2 #10 cans asparagus spears
1 quart Italian dressing

Marinate asparagus overnight in Italian dressing (refrigerated). Serve on top of tomato aspic square.

Vegetable Lasagna Rolls — 54 servings

3 pounds dry lasagna noodles (1 pound dry, app. 18 pieces)
1 #10 can tomatoes
2 quarts prepared spaghetti sauce
Extra basil, thyme, and oregano if desired
2 cups chopped green onions
4 pounds chopped spinach, cooked
2 pounds cottage cheese
2 cups shredded cheddar cheese
2 cups shredded Mozzarella cheese
2 cups grated Parmesan cheese
2 cups chopped parsley

Cook and drain noodles. Mix tomatoes, spaghetti sauce, and seasonings. Mix onions, spinach, and cheeses (except Parmesan). Spread noodles with cheese-spinach mixture and roll jelly-roll style. Place in a 12 × 20-inch pan seam side down. Pour tomato mixture over rolls. Cover and simmer for 30 minutes in oven at 350°. Uncover and sprinkle with Parmesan cheese and parsley. Serve, spooning sauce over each roll as served.

Sweet Potatoes in Orange Halves

2 #10 cans solid pack sweet potatoes
1 pound margarine, melted
2 tablespoons salt
4 cups light brown sugar
4 cups white sugar
1 quart half-and-half milk
2 pounds white raisins
50 large marshmallows
25 oranges, halved and scooped out, saving juice and pulp and leaving shells

Combine first 6 ingredients in mixer bowl and mix well. Add as much orange pulp and juice as desired, being careful not to thin mixture too much. Fold in raisins. Spoon mixture into orange shells. Bake in oven for 20 minutes at 350°. Remove from oven and top each orange half with a marshmallow. Return to oven and bake 10 minutes or until marshmallows are light brown.

Basic Tomato Aspic — 60 2-inch squares

8 6-ounce packages lemon flavored gelatin
2 #10 cans tomato juice
1 cup vinegar
2 tablespoons seasoned salt
2 tablespoons celery seed

Heat 1 can tomato juice. Dissolve gelatin in hot juice. Add cold juice and seasonings. Pour into 12 × 20-inch pan. Allow to gel. Serve topped with marinated asparagus spears. Add a strip of pimiento if desired for extra color.

VARIATION: Add chopped celery, green pepper, onion, nuts, cheese, olives, or other vegetables as desired.

DESSERTS

Because quality desserts are available commercially at a reasonable price, all desserts in this section utilize pre-prepared products. Included are desserts made from mixes, frozen, ready to eat, bakery desserts and desserts using more than one pre-prepared product. It is the author's purpose to encourage creative use of pre-prepared products to produce sumptuous desserts with little effort.

Carrot Cake

Several commercial pre-frosted carrot cakes are available frozen. Because of the nature of carrot cake batter, it retains a high level of flavor and texture. Look for familiar brand names when purchasing frozen carrot cake. For 50 luncheon size servings, plan to purchase 3–4 pounds.

Carrot cake mixes are included in the lines of all major manufacturers. Two supermarket size cake mixes will bake 1 18 × 26-inch sheet pan. One sheet will produce 50 servings 3¼ × 2½ inches.

Petits Fours

Petits fours may be made, using a baked sheet cake and covering all four sides of the cake with fondant; however, this requires a high degree of skill and a large amount of time. It is recommended that petits fours be purchased at a bakery. Petits fours are usually a bakery specialty and may be ordered in a shape, size, and color scheme suitable for any decor.

Ice Cream

A universal favorite, ice cream is perhaps the most useful prepared product for serving luncheons at church. A few tricks can transform ice cream into a festive and delicious dessert. One gallon of ice cream yields 32 ½-cup servings. For a luncheon serving 50, 1½ gallons should be the proper amount to purchase. Following are examples of creative treatment of ice cream.

Caramel Sundaes

Make generous use of prepared toppings for ice cream. One quart of caramel topping yields 64 tablespoons. To serve 50, plan to purchase 2 quarts for a generous topping. Scoop ice cream into serving dishes and spoon on the topping.

Ice-Cream Sandwiches

For 50 ice-cream sandwiches, purchase 100 soft oatmeal cookies and 1 gallon ice cream. Soften ice cream and portion onto a cookie with a #16 scoop. Top with a second cookie and refreeze quickly. Allow to thaw 10 minutes before serving.

Strawberry Parfait

For 50 strawberry parfaits, purchase 1 gallon vanilla or strawberry ice cream, 4 pounds sliced pre-sweetened strawberries, 2 16-ounce cartons of whipped topping, and 2 quarts of fresh whole strawberries. Layer into parfait glasses as follows: (1) ice cream, (2) sliced strawberries, (3) whipped topping. Top with one fresh whole strawberry (if available). Parfaits may be made up a day ahead of time and stored in the freezer (except for the fresh strawberry). Allow to soften for a few minutes before serving.

French Vanilla Ice Cream Balls

Soften French Vanilla ice cream and scoop into balls with a #8 scoop. Place balls on trays and freeze very hard. Toast 2 pounds shredded coconut and spread on trays. Quickly roll ice cream balls in coconut and return to freezer. May be served garnished with a cherry, dark chocolate shavings, or a colorful candy mint. For 50 servings, purchase 1½ gallons.

Sherbet

A universal favorite for luncheon desserts, this light colorful frozen dessert is available in a variety of flavors and colors. Sherbet is most attractive when portioned with a #8 scoop. Dipping the scoop into hot water between portions produces a smoother serving. Sherbet requires no garnish, but is made more festive with the addition of a sprig of fresh mint, an orange wedge, or a bit of candy in an appropriate shape or color.

EXAMPLE: Candy pumpkins for autumn, green mints for spring. For 50 servings, puchase 3 half gallons.

Frozen Yogurt

Frozen yogurt is just coming into its own as a choice for luncheon desserts. Because of its low fat content, frozen yogurt is becoming an accepted dessert for many group meals. More expensive than ice cream and sherbet, frozen yogurt is now available in a variety of flavors. Supermarkets usually offer frozen yogurt packed in quarts, and yogurt stores are located in shopping malls across the country. For an attractive luncheon dessert, handle frozen yogurt in the same manner suggested for sherbet. One quart yields 8 ½-cup servings.

Chocolate-Dipped Strawberries

For 50 servings, purchase 100 large fresh strawberries. Wash, leaving stems intact. Pat lightly with paper towels to dry. Soften 2 16-ounce cans of pre-prepared chocolate frosting in a saucepan over low heat, or in a fondue pot. Dip the lower half of each strawberry in the chocolate frosting and refrigerate quickly. Frosting will set and will hold its shape for serving. Strawberries may be dipped a second time if desired.

NOTE: Use chocolate frosting as a dip for other fruits as well. Mandarin oranges, apple slices, banana slices, and marshmallows are fun dippers for chocolate frosting. For a creative dessert, experiment with different fruits and different flavors of frosting.

Orange Danish Rolls

Orange Danish is just one example of a wide variety of yeast dough based products available in the supermarket dairy case. This suggestion is included because these products may be categorized as breakfast foods and overlooked as luncheon dessert possibilities. Orange Danish, usually packaged in 10's, includes pre-prepared orange frosting. Serve warm for best flavor and aroma.

Yeast dough products are also available frozen in a variety of forms and fillings. Fruit-filled turnovers, as well as cinnamon rolls, are dessert possibilities. Because they are purchased in individual servings, no waste is incurred.

Grasshopper Tarts

Tart shells are available in a variety of shapes and sizes. Packaged commercially in cases of 100 or more, this may not be a good choice for a luncheon unless tart shells can be utilized for another meal at church. Grasshopper tarts are suggested to make the consumer aware of chocolate tart shells.

For 50 grasshopper tarts, mix 5 6-ounce packages pistachio instant pudding according to package directions. Add ¼ cup peppermint extract and spoon into 50 3-inch chocolate tart shells. Just before serving, top with 1 tablespoon whipped topping. (Buy 2 16-ounce cartons whipped topping.)

Cherry Tarts

For 50 cherry tarts, purchase 50 3-inch regular pastry tart shells. Fill with prepared cherry pie filling (a 16-ounce jar fills 8 tarts). Cherry tarts may be served warm or cold. A spoonful of vanilla ice cream makes a warm tart extra special. One gallon of ice cream should be enough for 50.

Lemon Pie

Purchase 7 or 8 deep-dish shells and cook until light golden brown. Purchase 2 #10 cans prepared lemon pudding. Just before serving, fill pie shells and garnish with whipped topping. Cut in wedges, 7 servings per pie shell.

Cheese Cake

Cheese cake is a dessert easily prepared from a mix. Cheese cake is also available frozen, ready to eat. Both products are attractive and relatively inexpensive. Since cheese cake is a rich dessert, it may be served in small portions. Commerically prepared cheese cakes are usually sold in cases of 100 servings or more. Most supermarket cheese cake mixes yield 8 servings.

Trifle

Trifle may be served in 3 basic ways: (1) prepared and served from a punch bowl buffet style; (2) prepared in pans and served in sherbet dishes at the table; (3) prepared and served in individual dishes.

Ingredients for 50 servings of trifle are:

1½ gallons custard
3 16-ounce sponge cakes pulled into chunks (lady fingers, butter cake or sugar cookies may be used instead of sponge cake if desired).
1 quart raspberry or strawberry jam.
2 16-ounce cartons whipped topping

Layer into punch bowl or pan. Cake, jam, custard. Repeat layers. Top with whipped topping.

NOTE: Custard may be made with instant vanilla pudding, doubling the amount of milk in package directions. Added vanilla may also be desirable. If preparing individual trifles, use lady fingers instead of other cake choices.

Butterscotch Nut Squares

Layer ingredients as follows:

Layer 1
2 sticks margarine, melted
2 cups plain flour
2 cups chopped nuts

Press into 18 × 26-inch pan and bake in oven at 375° for 10 minutes. Cool.

Layer 2
1 pound cream cheese
2 cups powdered sugar
1 16-ounce carton whipped topping

Mix and spread over layer 1.

Layer 3
2 6-ounce packages instant butterscotch pudding mixed according to package directions

Spread over layer 2. Chill.

Layer 4
2 16-ounce packages whipped topping
2 cups graham cracker crumbs

Spread whipped topping over layer 3 and sprinkle graham cracker crumbs over top for garnish.

BREADS AND SANDWICHES

Buttermilk Biscuits — 1½-inch biscuits

4 cups self-rising flour
1 teaspoon baking soda
½ cup vegetable shortening
1½ cups buttermilk

Place flour and baking soda in a large bowl. Cut in shortening with a pastry cutter until it resembles coarse cornmeal. Add 1 cup buttermilk and mix with a large wooden spoon continuing to add a little buttermilk at a time until mixture forms a soft dough and leaves the sides of the bowl. Work with ½ of the dough at the time. Turn dough onto a floured surface and knead about 15 times. Roll with a rolling pin to about ½-inch thickness. Cut with a biscuit cutter and bake in oven at 425° for 12 to 15 minutes. Biscuits may be split and buttered before serving if desired.

VARIATIONS:

CHEESE BISCUITS—Add 1½ cups shredded cheddar cheese to flour and cut into dough with shortening. Mix and bake as above (Makes approximately 6 extra biscuits.)

WHOLE WHEAT BISCUITS—Use half wheat flour and half white self-rising flour. Add 1 tablespoon baking powder and 1 teaspoon salt. Mix and bake as above.

NOTE: HOW TO KNEAD BISCUIT DOUGH—Form dough into a flat ball. Place on floured surface. Use both hands. Grasp back side of ball and fold dough in half toward you. Knead folded ball with both hands, pushing away from you. Turn ball of dough 180° and repeat the process as many times as necessary to produce a smooth well-mixed ball that is not sticky and rolls easily into proper thickness for biscuits.

Bran Muffins — small muffins

1 cup vegetable oil
3 cups sugar
4 eggs, beaten
6 cups 100% bran breakfast cereal
1½ cups hot water
5 cups self-rising flour
1 tablespoon baking soda
4 cups buttermilk

Mix oil, sugar, and eggs. Mix bran cereal and hot water and add to first mixture. Combine baking soda with flour and add alternately with buttermilk. Stir just enough to mix all ingredients. Fill greased muffin tins ⅔ full (app. ¼ c. batter per muffin) and bake at 400° for 20 minutes.

VARIATION: Raisin Bran Muffins—Soak 2 cups raisins in boiling water until they are plumped. Drain. Add to batter last. Bake as above.

Mix for Fruit and Nut Breads

This recipe is used here because of the wide variety of recipes which may be developed from it. Three variations are given below, but any fruits or nuts desired may be added, using the general directions below. If stored, mix should be placed in air-tight containers or bags and kept in a cool place.

3½ cups self-rising flour
1 cup nonfat dry milk powder
¾ cup sugar
½ cup vegetable shortening

Cut with pastry blender until shortening is well mixed with other ingredients.

Banana Bread — 2 large loaves

1 recipe mix (as given above)
2 eggs
1½ cups water
¼ cup vegetable oil
3 large bananas, mashed

Combine all ingredients gently, stirring just enough to incorporate flour mixture into other ingredients. Bake in greased loaf pans at 350° for 50 minutes or until bread leaves sides of pan and center of loaf springs back from a touch.

Cranberry Bread

Substitute 1 16-ounce can jellied whole cranberry sauce for the bananas. Mix and bake as above.

Pumpkin Bread

Substitute 2 cups cooked pumpkin for bananas. Add spices as desired. Mix and bake as above.

Yeast Rolls — 2-inch rolls

2 packages dry yeast
1 cup warm water
6–7 cups sifted plain flour
2 teaspoons salt
½ cup sugar
2 eggs
1 cup vegetable shortening, melted
1 cup cold water

Dissolve yeast in warm water. Combine flour, salt, and sugar in large bowl. Make a well in center and add other ingredients. Stir with a large wooden spoon until well mixed. Cover and allow to rise for 3–4 hours. Knead and work dough until it is glossy. Roll and cut into desired shape. Cover and allow to rise until double in bulk. Bake at 450° until lightly brown.

Cucumber Sandwiches

1 large cucumber grated or processed in food processor
2 6-ounce packages cream cheese, softened
1 teaspoon Worcestershire sauce

Mix all ingredients and spread on whole wheat or white bread from which crusts have been removed. Cut into desired shapes. Serve open or closed faced.

Toasted Open-Faced Cheese Sandwiches

Remove crusts from 50 slices white or wheat bread. Place bread slices on an 18 × 26-inch baking sheet (one sheet will hold 48 slices). Spread each slice with mayonnaise and top with a 1-ounce slice American cheese, or American style cheese food. Place pan in oven at 300° and toast until bread is lightly browned and cheese is melted (app. 10 minutes). Serve immediately.

Menus for Youth and Children's Functions

Fifty Servings

NOTE: Since children and teens are often involved in preparation of food for their church groups, menus have been kept as simple as possible. It is suggested that bakery bread, crackers, and cookies, fresh fruits, and ice cream, be used in preparing meals for young people. Recipes for major items are in quantity for serving 50. Any of these recipes may be successfully cut in half for serving 25.

Homemade Chili
Cheese and Crackers
Fruit Wedges

Ravioli Casserole
Green Salad
Texas Toast

Barbecued Franks
Sweet Sour Slaw   Baked Beans
Buns

Crock Pot Hot Dogs with Chili
Corn Chips
Buns

Fancy Burgers
Potato Chips or Oven Fries

Sloppy Joe on Buns
Fresh Fruit

French Bread Pizza—Ready-to-Bake Pizza
—Frozen Individual Pizza—
Deep-Dish Homemade Pizza
Green Salad

Jumbo Tacos
Stuffed Celery

Taco Salads
Extra Chips
Apple Halves

Burritos with Chili and Cheese
Crunchy Vegetables and Dip

Chicken Sandwiches with Lettuce and Tomato
(Made with chicken nuggets, planks, or patties)
Oven Potatoes

POTATO BAR WITH TOPPINGS

Select large baking potatoes. Scrub and pierce skin with fork. Bake in oven at 350° until potatoes are tender. Baking time will vary with number of potatoes and type of oven. Allow at least one hour.

Suggested toppings: Chili, baked beans, chopped ham, chopped franks, hard-cooked egg, spaghetti sauce, barbecue sauce, crunchy vegetables, butter, sour cream, buttermilk dressing.

SALAD BAR

Prepare salad greens in a large bowl. Lettuce, spinach, cabbage or combinations of these are suggested.

Suggested toppings: fresh tomatoes, green peppers, cucumbers, onion rings, canned corn, canned pork and beans, cottage cheese, American cheese, chopped ham or luncheon meats, bacon bits.

BUILD YOUR OWN SANDWICH BAR

Suggested plan: Provide a variety of breads, cold sliced meats, cheese, and pickles, along with lettuce, tomato and a variety of dressings. Expect creativity!

Menus and Snacks for Outdoor Activities

Fifty Servings

SUMMER CAMPOUT

Hobo Dinners
Whole Wheat Rolls
Traveling Salad

AUTUMN HIKE

Lunch-Box Chili Dogs
Space-Age Manna

FOOTBALL PICNIC

Tailgate Tacos
Whole Oranges

WIENER ROAST

Roasted Wieners on Buns with Trimmings
Roasted Apples
Roasted Marshmallows

SUMMER ICE CREAM PARTY

Bring Your Own Sandwich
Homemade Ice Cream Kid Style

PICNIC IN THE PARK

Giant Deli Sandwiches
Assorted Fresh Fruits

Recipes for Youth and Children's Functions

Fifty Servings

Beef Ravioli Casserole

4 pounds lean ground beef
2 #10 cans beef mini ravioli
2 pounds shredded cheddar cheese (or mix with mozzarella)

Brown beef in serving pans. Drain off excess fat. Remove half of browned beef from each pan and set aside. Pour two cans mini ravioli into each pan on top of the layer of beef. Spread cheese generously over the ravioli. Add the remaining beef and top with remaining cheese. Bake in oven at 325° for 20–30 minutes until cheese is melted and pans are bubbling.

NOTE: For extra flavor, add 2 cups chopped onion per pan.

Hobo Dinners

For each dinner, use 4 ounces lean ground beef made into patty, 1 medium potato sliced (peeling left on), 1 large carrot scraped and sliced into ¼-inch coins, one generous slice of onion, salt and pepper or other seasonings as desired.

Tear a 12-inch square of aluminum foil for each dinner. Place meat patty in center of square. Top with sliced potato, carrot, and onion. Season as desired. Bring corners of foil together, sealing tightly. Bake in campfire ashes for 30 minutes. Serve in foil with bread and fresh fruit. For 50 hobo dinners you will need the following:

12½ pounds ground beef
16 pounds white potatoes
5 pounds carrots
3 pounds onions

Chili

4 pounds lean ground beef
10 large onions, chopped
10 cloves garlic, minced
4 cups water
1 #10 can tomatoes
2 #10 cans red kidney beans
2 tablespoons chili powder
½ teaspoon ground red pepper (optional)

Brown ground beef and drain off fat. Add water, onions, and garlic. Simmer in a large kettle for 2 hours, adding more water if mixture becomes dry. Add tomatoes, beans, and seasonings and simmer 1 additional hour. If mixture is too thick, add water or tomato juice, and simmer 15 minutes longer.

NOTE: Cut this recipe in half for serving chili with hot dogs, burritos, and for Tailgate Tacos.

Lunch-Box Chili Dogs

Ask each participant to bring a lunch-box size thermos. Fill each thermos with hot chili. Suspend a 2-ounce wiener inside each thermos of chili, using an 18-inch strand of dental floss. Leave enough dental floss outside so that when lid is unscrewed, wiener may be retrieved. Youth sponsors produce a bun and plenty of napkins for each participant.

Tailgate Tacos

Purchase corn chips in individual bags. Sponsors bring along chili, allowing ½ cup per person. At serving time, pass out the corn-chip bags, open, and spoon chili into bag with chips. Provide plastic spoons.

NOTE: If serving fresh oranges with Tailgate Tacos, prepare them for easy peeling by immersing oranges in boiling water for 20 seconds.

Burgers

1 pound lean ground beef for each 4 giant burgers
Salt, pepper and other seasonings as desired

Shape hamburger patties by hand, using 4 ounces lean ground beef. Season patties with salt, pepper, and garlic salt and cook on ungreased griddle or braising pan. Do not turn patties until bottom surface has browned to prevent sticking. Try the following fancy trimmings for giant burgers.

Place a pineapple ring on top of each patty just before removing from griddle. Add a #10 can of mushrooms to pan and allow to heat. Serve a spoonful of mushrooms on each burger. Top each burger with a slice of Swiss cheese. Serve when cheese is softened and has taken the shape of the meat. Add chopped onion and chopped green pepper to the pan. When softened, serve spooned over the meat pattie. For an extra special burger, combine the last two suggestions for a Swiss and onion pepper burger.

Sloppy Joe Burgers

6 pounds lean ground beef
4 medium onions, chopped
3 cloves garlic, minced
2 celery stalks, finely chopped
1 tablespoon salt

1 teaspoon black pepper
3 tablespoons Worcestershire sauce
1 24-ounce bottle tomato catsup

Brown beef, onions, garlic, and celery in large pot or braising pan. Add seasonings and catsup and simmer for 30 minutes. Portion with a #16 scoop onto hot buns.

Pizza — 4 × 6-inch servings

Although pizza is available in a wide variety of shapes, styles, and forms, only one basic pizza recipe will be included. Following the pizza recipe, product and purchasing suggestions will be made to inform youth sponsors and other church personnel who wish to include this popular menu item in church functions.

Deep-Dish Pizza

Yeast dough crust prepared from ½ Hot Roll recipe (page 114)
Roll dough thin into 2 18 × 26-inch pans

5 pounds ground beef, browned and drained
1 quart tomato paste
1 tablespoon ground oregano
1 teaspoon garlic powder
⅓ cup sugar
3 pounds Mozzarella cheese

Mix browned beef, tomato paste and seasonings and spread over pizza crust (about 1½ quart on each pan). Bake at 425° for 10 minutes. Remove from oven and top with shredded cheese. Lower heat to 300° and cook 5 more minutes.

VARIATIONS: Add pepperoni, black olives, green pepper, onion, anchovies, capers, or other toppings as desired. Sausage may be mixed with or substituted for ground beef.

CRUST VARIATION: Cook pizza mixture above for 20 minutes on top of range. Spoon cooked mixture onto split French Rolls. Top with cheese and toast in hot oven until cheese is melted.

Pre-prepared pizza crust is available in 18 × 26-inch sheets. Prepare as above.

Purchased Pizza

Following are the more popular forms of precooked pizza available in the food service market. Your salesman may suggest others.

5-inch deep-dish individual pizzas
Pizza wedges
Individual pizza rectangles
9-inch, 10-inch and 14-inch round uncut pizzas
Individual boat shaped pizzas for less spillage of fillings

Ready to bake pizzas may be made to order and purchased ready for your oven.

Ready baked pizzas may be ordered and delivered to your group hot and ready to eat.

Burritos

With the increase in popularity of Mexican foods, the burrito has become almost as popular with youth groups as pizza. Burritos are inexpensive and may be purchased in the supermarket or from quantity food service vendors and are usually packaged 72 in a case.

Frankfurters and Variations

Frankfurters, wieners, and hot dogs are usually interchangeable terms when preparing food for groups of young people. These products have a wide range in price because of ingredient content. Some good ones are inexpensive, but some cheap ones are not good. One way to purchase a quality product at a low price is to choose those made from chicken or turkey instead of beef or pork. Choose products made by a reputable poultry products manufacturer and read the label for content. Too much cereal filler makes a poor product, as well as excessive use of meat byproducts. Supermarket packages usually contain 8 or 10 units, 1½ ounces or 2 ounces each. Bulk packages of 36 or 100 may also be available.

Oven-Barbecued Franks

50 2-ounce frankfurters
1 quart barbecue sauce

Spread franks in a 12 × 2 × 2-inch pan. Add barbecue sauce and bake in oven at 350° for 30 minutes or until franks are puffy and brown on top. Serve at once.

Crock Pot Hot Dogs

50 2-ounce wieners

Use traditional crock pot or covered 12 × 20-inch pan on range top at very low setting. Cook for 1 hour or until hot dogs are puffy and tender. Serve at once.

Sweet and Sour Wieners

50 2-ounce wieners
1 quart prepared sweet and sour sauce

Cut wieners into bite-size pieces. Add sweet and sour sauce. Bake in oven at 350° until browned and puffy.

Tacos

15 pounds ground beef
6 large onions, chopped
4 tablespoons chili powder
3 cups tomato paste
2 large heads lettuce, shredded
5 pounds cheddar cheese
20 medium tomatoes, chopped
50 jumbo taco shells
Prepared taco sauce as desired

Brown ground beef and onion in a 12 × 20-inch pan. Drain. Add tomato paste and chili powder and simmer for 15–30 minutes. While meat is simmering, prepare lettuce, cheese and tomatoes and mix these in a 2 × 2-inch pan.

Assemble tacos as follows: Use a #16 scoop. Into each shell place one scoop of meat and one scoop of vegetable-cheese mixture. Top with taco sauce as desired.

Taco Salads

For each salad, use ¾ cup corn chips, ½ cup canned chili with beans, ¼ cup shredded lettuce, ¼ cup shredded cheese, and 1 tablespoon sour cream. Assemble as follows: layer 1, corn chips; layer 2, chili; layer 3, shredded lettuce; layer 4, shredded cheese; layer 5, sour cream.

For 50 Taco Salads you will need the following:

5 1-pound bags corn chips
2 #10 cans chili
2 medium heads lettuce
2 pounds shredded cheese
3 1-pound cartons sour cream

Giant Deli Sandwiches

2 giant loaves (60-inch) bread, sliced lengthwise
3 pounds assorted sandwich meats, sliced thin
3 pounds assorted cheeses, sliced thin
6 firm tomatoes, sliced thin
1 bunch leaf lettuce
1 bunch raw spinach
1 pint alfalfa sprouts
1 pint each sweet and dill pickle slices
½ pint each mayonnaise, mustard, and catsup

Spread upper and lower halves of bread with mustard, mayonnaise, and catsup at various locations on the loaf of bread. Arrange sandwich ingredients randomly on bread. Wrap giant sandwiches in foil and transport to picnic location. When ready to serve, allow each picnic participant to select location for cutting his sandwich. One 60-inch loaf will serve 20–25.

Traveling Salad

Lettuce leaves (1 for each salad desired)
Peanut butter (1 T. for each salad)
Celery (1 T. chopped for each salad)
Raisins (1 T. chopped for each salad)
Miniature marshmallows (1 T. for each salad)

Spread lettuce leaves generously with peanut butter. Add other ingredients. Roll lettuce leaf around ingredients, allowing peanut butter to hold salad together. Tuck in edges of leaf to make a neat package, adding peanut butter if necessary to hold package together.

Space-Age Manna

2 16-ounce boxes sweetened breakfast cereal
1 16-ounce package chocolate chips
1 16-ounce package butterscotch chips
1 16-ounce package raisins
1 16-ounce can dry roasted peanuts
1 16-ounce can mixed salted nuts

Mix in large container and portion into zip-top plastic bags for individual servings.

Roasting Wieners, Apples and Marshmallows

Roasted Wieners—Select 2 ounces wieners for better flavor and texture of roasted product.

Roasted Apples—Select small to medium apples for best results. Peel apples just before roasting. Roast over hot coals until apple begins to soften. Mix one pound of white granulated sugar with 1 tablespoon cinnamon in a metal bowl. As apples are roasted, roll in sugar and cinnamon mixture.

Roasted Marshmallows—For an extra color treat, select large pastel colored marshmallows for roasting.

Homemade Ice Cream Kid Style — 6 ½-cup servings

2 cups whole milk
1 egg, well beaten
¾ cup sugar
1 teaspoon vanilla
1 1-pound coffee can with plastic lid
1 #10 can with plastic lid
Masking tape
1 cup ice cream salt
Crushed ice

Mix ingredients. Pour into coffee can. Seal very firmly with masking tape. Set coffee can inside #10 can. Pack with salt and ice. Cover with plastic lid and seal tight with masking tape. Plan a relay game where children roll sealed can on a smooth surface for 20 minutes. When cans are opened, ice cream is made.

Sweet Sour Slaw — ½-cup servings

2 large heads cabbage, shredded
1 pound red radishes, sliced thin
2 large onions, chopped fine
1 large green cucumber, sliced thin
1 pound carrots, sliced thin
1 cup vegetable oil
1 cup sugar
1 cup white vinegar
1 tablespoon celery seed

Prepare vegetables and mix lightly. Mix oil, sugar, vinegar, and celery seed. Pour over vegetables and allow to set for 1 hour.

Easy Baked Beans — ½-cup servings

2 #10 cans pork and beans
2 cups catsup
2 cups dark corn syrup
½ cup prepared mustard
½ cup Worcestershire sauce
1 pound sliced bacon

Mix beans and seasonings in a 12 × 20 × 4-inch pan. Place bacon slices on top. Bake in oven at 350° for 45 minutes or until bacon is crisp and beans are thick and bubbly.

Green Salad for Fifty—½ recipe in section for All-Church Fellowship Dinners.

Desserts Children and Teens Can Prepare (With Supervision)

Teens Build Your Own Sundae Party

Suggested plan: Provide containers of favorite flavors of ice cream, and assorted prepared toppings. Some favorite toppings include chocolate, caramel, pineapple, and strawberry. Provide large cartons of whipped toppings, cherries, banana slices, nuts and crushed peppermint sticks. For serving, use #8 scoops. Buy twice as much ice cream as you think you need.

Campfire Bananas

1 large banana per person
Miniature marshmallows
Butterscotch chips
Raisins

Peel one strip from the inside curve of a large banana. Do not remove. Scoop out about half of the banana inside. Fill cavity with marshmallows, chips and raisins. Replace peeling strip. Wrap bananas in foil and place in warm ashes of campfire while devotional (or other activity) is in progress. Serve one foil package for each person. Provide a plastic spoon.

Homemade Lollipops

This activity should be attempted only if ample adult supervision is available because of the danger from burns. The lollipop mixture is very hot and must be handled quickly. If sponsors are brave enough, assemble the following:

Cookie cutters in desired shapes (well oiled)
Lollipop or popsicle sticks
Plastic wrap
Hard candies, or other desired decorations
1 tube cake decorator icing
Candy thermometer

Lollipop Recipe — Yields 6 medium lollipops

1 cup sugar
⅓ cup light corn syrup
¼ cup water
½ teaspoon peppermint or lemon extract
Food coloring as desired

Combine ingredients in a saucepan. Stir over medium heat until sugar dissolves. Cook without stirring until mixture reaches 310° on a candy thermometer. Pour at once into prepared cookie cutters. Do not use all the mixture. Save about 2 tablespoons for attaching lollipop sticks later. Allow lollipops to harden in the cookie cutters. When mixture is solid, reheat reserved lollipop mixture until it is liquid. Tilt cookie cutters and lay sticks on tilted edge of cutter. Pour enough liquid mixture to attach sticks to original lollipop. When lollipops have hardened, loosen from cookie cutters, decorate as desired, using a tube of prepared cake decorator icing to attach decorations. Wrap in plastic wrap and decorate sticks with appropriate bows or decorations.

Caramel Pop Corn Party

1 cup dark corn syrup
1 cup white sugar
½ cup white corn syrup
2 sticks margarine
1 teaspoon soda
16 cups popped corn
Nuts as desired

Boil sugar, syrups and margarine for 5 minutes. Remove from heat and stir in soda. Add nuts if desired. Pour over popped corn and stir well. Turn into large greased pan and bake in oven at 200° for 45 minutes, stirring every 15 minutes.

Decorating Tips for Parties, Receptions and Teas

TABLE COVERS

Although a wide variety of decorated paper table coverings are available, a party is more elegant and festive if fabric table cloths are used instead of paper ones. Linen tablecloths are quite expensive and difficult to launder. Some wash-and-wear table linens are attractive and relatively inexpensive. Some churches may wish to invest in table linens to be used for church functions.

If church-owned table linens are not available, try some of the following nontraditional table coverings for church parties, receptions, and teas.

1. Pastel or dark bright sheets
2. Drapery fabrics in 60-inch widths (usually treated to be water resistant)
3. Giant beach towels
4. Grandma's country quilts (sprayed heavily with water-resistant treatment)
5. Lengths of craft fabrics printed with appropriate holiday or special occasion motif.

TABLE DECORATIONS

Fresh flowers add an elegant touch, but are not necessary for most parties at church. An arrangement of silk flowers is usually easy to borrow from a church member. Most larger supermarkets now offer fresh flowers and potted plants at a fraction of florist cost.

Table decorations abound in gardens, yards, and homes of church members. Consider the following:

1. Red apples for Valentine, Independence Day, Autumn, Thanksgiving or Christmas.
2. Plastic or garage sale baskets painted in matching colors. Fill them with flowers, leaves, fruits, vegetables, children's stuffed toys, eggs, decorative candies, cookies, or loaves of bread.
3. Clear glass jars decorated and/or filled may be arranged randomly on tables with one large brandy snifter, aquarium, or terrarium used for a head table decoration.
4. Antique (or new) kitchen tools, each one resting on a colored place mat, are appropriate decorations for a kitchen shower, homecoming dinner, or women's luncheon.
5. Use dolls in ethnic costume for international or missions related functions.
6. Gourds, squash, eggplants, cucumbers, and corn are usually available at a low cost and are especially attractive decorations for late summer and autumn functions.
7. Grapevine, honeysuckle, ivy and sumac are often overlooked as table decoration possibilities.
8. Toy automobiles borrowed from children create an attractive table for men and boys' functions.
9. Lemons and grapefruit combined with greenery create a festive Spring table.
10. Use baby dolls to decorate for a baby shower.

IDEAS FOR PLACE FAVORS, OR PLACE-CARD HOLDERS

1. Decorated eggs
2. Candy canes, hearts, rabbits, strawberries, corn, or any appropriate shape
3. Candy mint patties or lollipops
4. Decorated cookies
5. Baby food jars, decorated and filled
6. Lemons, small apples, tangerines, or other small fruit decorated with edible paints
7. Colored souffle cups filled with caramel popcorn, candies or nuts
8. Decorated pine cones, buckeyes, acorns, or chestnuts
9. Spools from sewing thread painted, ribbon trimmed and used to hold small candles
10. Small plants potted in paper cups
11. Decorated clothes pins
12. Christmas tree ornaments
13. Single fresh, dried, or silk flowers with ribbon decorated stem
14. Small decorative soaps
15. Perfume samples (often available from department stores)

Recipes for Party Foods

HOT AND COLD BEVERAGES

Autumn Spice Punch — Serves 24–30

1 cup sugar
1 teaspoon cinnamon
1 tablespoon lemon juice
2 cups boiling water
2 46-ounce cans pineapple juice
1 32-ounce can cranberry juice
1 32-ounce can apple juice
1 2-liter bottle ginger ale

Make syrup of first 4 ingredients. Chill. Pour into punch bowl. Add chilled juices, ginger ale and ice ring. Garnish each cup with mint leaves if desired.

Making an Ice Ring

Freeze water or one ingredient of punch in a round mold or tube pan. Add mint leaves, lemon slices, cherries or other garnishes to liquid and freeze in the ring.

Banana Punch — Serves 24–30

4 cups sugar
8 cups water
5 bananas, mashed
½ cup lemon juice
1 46-ounce can frozen orange juice concentrate
½ gallon pineapple sherbet, softened

Make syrup from sugar and water. Boil 5 minutes. Cool. Mix lemon juice and mashed bananas. Pour above mixtures into punch bowl. Add pineapple juice and orange concentrate. Add sherbet just before serving.

Bubbly Holiday Egg Nog — Serves 24–30

6 eggs
1 cup sugar
¼ teaspoon cinnamon, ground
¼ teaspoon ginger, ground
2 12-ounce cans frozen orange juice concentrate (reconstituted)
½ cup lemon juice
1 quart French Vanilla ice cream
1 2-liter bottle ginger ale

Combine eggs, sugar and spices in food processor. Mix well. Pour juices into punch bowl. Add egg mixture and blend. Add softened ice cream. Pour in ginger ale just before serving. Sprinkle nutmeg on top if desired.

Fruit Tea — Yields 16 tall glasses

1 quart boiling water
12 small tea bags
Juice of 4 oranges
Juice of 4 lemons
2 cups sugar
3 quarts cold water

Pour boiling water over tea bags and steep for 5 minutes. Combine fruit juices, sugar, and cold water. Add tea. Serve over crushed ice garnished with mint leaves.

Hot Chocolate Punch — Serves 20

1 gallon dairy chocolate milk
2 large cartons prepared whipped topping
Shaved chocolate
Peppermint sticks

Heat chocolate milk to 180°. Pour into warmed punch bowl. Garnish with dollops of whipped topping. Sprinkle shaved chocolate over top of whipped topping. Serve in punch cups, using a peppermint stick for stirring.

Instant Spiced Tea — Yields 60 6-ounce cups

1 cup instant orange flavored breakfast drink
1 6½-ounce package lemonade mix
½ cup unsweetened instant tea
1 teaspoon cinnamon
1 teaspoon cloves
1 cup sugar

Mix together. Use 2 teaspoons per 6-ounce cup of hot water.

Lemon Punch — Serves 24–30

2 6-ounce cans frozen lemonade concentrate
2 6-ounce cans frozen pineapple juice concentrate
3 quarts water
2 2-liter bottles ginger ale

Mix juice concentrates and water. Pour over ice ring in punch bowl. Add ginger ale last.

Vegetable Juice Slush — Serves 16

2 46-ounce cans vegetable juice cocktail
2 tablespoons lemon juice
½ teaspoon hot pepper sauce

Pour into shallow pan and freeze until slushy. Spoon into juice glasses and garnish with a lemon slice.

Wassail — Serves 16

1 64-ounce bottle cranberry juice
1 64-ounce bottle apple juice
1 cup white corn syrup
1 tablespoon whole cloves
3 whole cinnamon sticks

Combine juices and syrup in large container. Tie spices in a cheese cloth square and add spice bag to juice mixture. Bring to a boil then reduce heat. Simmer for 30 minutes. Remove spice bag and serve beverage warm.

DIPS

A wide variety of dips are available already mixed, but most are quite expensive. At least half the cost may be saved by mixing dips yourself.

Fresh vegetables, fruits, chips, and crackers offer a wide variety of dippers. Following are examples of dips in a variety of flavors. Creativity is the key word in mixing dips and dippers as successful party foods.

It is difficult to calculate the number of servings dip recipes will yield since guests serve themselves. For this reason, no serving yield is given with dip recipes.

Chicken a la King Dip

1 6-ounce package cream cheese
1 12-ounce can cream of mushroom soup
1 tablespoon onion powder
1 teaspoon dried parsley flakes
1 tablespoon chopped pimiento
2 6-ounce cans deboned chicken

Melt cheese in double boiler. Add soup and seasonings. Mix in pimiento and chicken. Heat to 180°. Do not boil. Serve in chafing dish with chips and crackers.

Cucumber Dip

2 cups cottage cheese
1 medium cucumber
4 green onions, chopped
Juice of 1 lemon
2 teaspoons seasoned salt
2 large white radishes
¼ teaspoon hot pepper sauce

Process all ingredients together in food processor until smooth. Chill. Serve with assorted crackers.

Fruit Dip

2 16-ounce jars marshmallow cream
1 3-ounce package cream cheese
2 tablespoons milk
3 drops red food color (optional)

Soften cream cheese and blend into marshmallow cream. Thin with milk to desired consistency. Add food color (optional). Serve with fresh strawberries, grapes, pineapple chunks, and apple slices.

Mayonnaise Dip for Vegetables

2 cups mayonnaise
½ cup minced fresh parsley (or ¼ c. dried parsley)
½ cup minced onion
1 teaspoon Worcestershire sauce
¼ teaspoon seasoned pepper
1 cup buttermilk

Mix and chill. Use carrot sticks, celery sticks, broccoli spears, caulifowerets, radishes, or cucumber slices as dippers.

Mexican Salsa

2½ cups finely chopped fresh tomatoes
2 garlic cloves, minced
½ cup chopped green onions
½ cup chopped fresh parsley
½ cup minced green chili peppers (canned)
½ minced green sweet pepper
1 teaspoon minced fresh oregano or ½ teaspoon dried oregano
1 teaspoon salt
2 tablespoons cooking oil
1 tablespoon lemon juice
1 teaspoon hot pepper sauce if desired

Mix and chill for several hours before serving. Serve with tortilla chips.

HOT HORS D'OEUVRES

Bacon Crunchies — Yields about 36 crunchies

1 pound thin sliced bacon
Rectangular shaped party crackers

Wrap one slice (room temperature) bacon around one cracker. Pin with a tooth pick. Bake in oven at 400° for 10 minutes or until bacon is crisp.

Cinnamon Toast Sandwiches — Yields about 24

Trim crusts from very fresh white bread. Spread slices with a paste made from 1 cup brown sugar, 2 tablespoons melted butter and 1 teaspoon cinnamon. Roll jelly roll style and brush outsides with melted butter. Toast. Serve hot. (May be made ahead and toasted just before serving time.)

Clam Fritters — Makes 30 fritters

2 6½-ounce cans chopped clams, drained (reserve ½ c. liquid)
2 eggs
½ cup milk
2 tablespoons vegetable oil
2 cups self-rising flour
Vegetable oil for frying

Beat eggs, milk, clam liquid, and vegetable oil in large mixer bowl. Add flour and mix well. Add clams and mix lightly. Deep fry in oil at 375°, dropping by teaspoons into oil and frying until golden. Drain. Serve hot.

Clam Roll-Ups — Makes 32 rolls

2 6½-ounce cans minced clams, drained
½ cup mayonnaise
1 tablespoon grated onion
½ teaspoon curry powder
8 slices very fresh white bread (crusts removed)
Melted butter or margarine

Combine clams, mayonnaise, onion, and curry powder. Flatten bread slices with rolling pin. Spread bread slices with clam mixture, 2 tablespoons per slice. Roll jelly roll style. Brush with butter and refrigerate or freeze. When ready to serve, cut each roll in 4 slices. Bake at 450° for 8 minutes or until golden brown. Serve hot.

Individual Pizzas — Yield about 24

1 pound ground chuck
1 medium onion, finely chopped
1 teaspoon ground oregano
12 ounces shredded mozzarella cheese
1 cup pre-prepared spaghetti sauce
24 slices party rye bread

Brown meat, onion, and oregano. Mix in the spaghetti sauce and spoon onto slices of party rye bread. Top with shredded cheese and bake in oven at 350° for 5–7 minutes or until bread has toasted and cheese has melted. Serve hot.

Little English Pizzas — Yields 48

1 pound mozzarella cheese
6 tender green onions
10 stuffed olives
½ cup tomato catsup
1 tablespoon Worcestershire sauce
1½ teaspoon oregano
½ teaspoon hot pepper sauce
6 English Muffins (sourdough style)

Place all ingredients in a food processor. Chop, being careful not to overprocess. Onions and olives should be chopped but retain their identity in the mixture. Spread on English muffin halves. Broil until bubbly and slightly brown. Cut into bite-size tidbits.

Orange Marmalade Toast Rounds

Cut rounds from white bread with small biscuit cutter. Spread with melted butter and orange marmalade. Sprinkle with grated American cheese and toast under broiler. Serve hot.

Oriental Chicken Wings — Yields 36 pieces

18 chicken wings
½ cup soy sauce
1 cup dark brown sugar

Cut off wing tips and cut wings into two pieces, separating at the joint. Put wing pieces in a 12 × 20-inch pan. Mix sugar and soy sauce and pour over wings. Bake in oven at 325° for 30 minutes. Turn each wing piece. Increase the oven temperature to 375° and bake for 20 minutes or until wings are tender and slightly crisp.

Stuffed Mushrooms — Yields 24 medium mushrooms

Mushrooms (small to medium size)
Melted butter or margarine
½ cup celery, chopped
Vegetable oil for sauteeing
2 6½-ounce cans deviled ham

Remove mushroom stems and chop fine. Mix chopped stems with celery and sautee in a little oil until tender. Mix with deviled ham. Spoon into mushroom caps which have been brushed with butter. Bake in oven at 400° for 7 minutes or until mushrooms are tender.

VARIATION: Mushrooms may be stuffed with chicken salad, seasoned stuffing mix, hot pork sausage, or your favorite pre-prepared spread.

PARTY SANDWICHES

When making sandwiches for a party, remember that bread dries out quickly. Always have fillings ready before removing bread from its wrapper. Work fast.

To prevent sandwich fillings from soaking into bread and making it soggy, spread slices of bread with butter, margarine or mayonnaise before spreading sandwich filling.

Remember to spread sandwich fillings to the edges of bread to prevent dry edges.

Line a shallow pan with a damp towel, then with waxed paper. Separate each layer of sandwiches with waxed paper. Cover top layer with waxed paper and another damp towel. Refrigerate until serving time.

Rolled Asparagus Sandwiches

1 #2½ can green asparagus spears
20 slices white or wheat bread (crusts removed)
Sweet hot mustard
Italian dressing

Marinate asparagus spears in Italian dressing for several hours. Spread bread slices with sweet hot mustard. Roll each spear of asparagus in a slice of bread and secure with tooth picks. Arrange on a tray like spokes of a wheel. Center tray with cherry tomatoes.

NOTE: These sandwiches may also be toasted and served hot.

Chicken Salad for Sandwiches

Yields 24 party sandwiches

4 whole chicken breasts, cooked and deboned
¾ cup finely chopped celery
2 tablespoons finely chopped sweet pickle
2 hard-cooked eggs, chopped
¼ cup toasted pecans
1 tablespoon lemon juice
1 teaspoon salt
¾ cup mayonnaise

Process chicken meat in food processor until coarsely chopped. Add other ingredients and process a few more seconds to mix. Do not overprocess. Ingredients should retain their identity.

VARIATION: 2 6½-ounce cans white chunk tuna may be substituted for the chicken with equally tasty results.

Cream Cheese Sandwiches

Cream cheese is the basic ingredient for most party sandwiches. Cream cheese combines well with fruits and vegetables and enhances the flavor of fruit and nut breads. It becomes light and fluffy when whipped. Generally speaking, 1 6-ounce package of cream cheese combined with one other ingredient makes about 20 party sandwiches. Following is a list of ingredients to combine with 1 6-ounce package of cream cheese.

¼ cup chopped maraschino cherries
¼ cup honey
¼ cup cranberry sauce
¼ cup chopped dates
¼ cup strawberry jam
¼ cup mincemeat
2 tablespoons minced onion and 2 tablespoons chopped green pepper
12 chopped stuffed olives
¼ cup chopped cucumber
¼ cup chopped fresh parsley
¼ cup crumbled crisp bacon
¼ cup chopped toasted pecans

Cream cheese may be sandwiched between two slices of bread or served open-faced with an endless variety of garnishes. Following are suggested garnishes:

Parsley
Nut halves
Cherry tomatoes
Maraschino cherries
Paprika
Vegetable tidbits
Raw onion rings
Green pepper strips
Pimiento strips

PARTY FRUIT AND NUT BREADS

Apricot Orange Bread — Yields 12–14 slices

1 cup dried apricots
1 cup sugar
2 tablespoons soft margarine
1 egg
Juice and grated rind of one orange
Water to make ¾-cup liquid
2 cups plain flour
2 teaspoons baking powder
1 teaspoon salt
½ cup chopped nuts

Cover apricots in warm water and soak 30 minutes. Drain and cut with scissors into small pieces. Cream sugar and butter. Add egg. Add water and juice. Sift dry ingredients together and add to above mixture. Blend in nuts and apricots. Pour into 9 × 5 × 2-inch pan that has been greased and dredged with flour. Bake in oven at 350° for 55–60 minutes or until edges begin to loosen from pan and top is golden brown. Cool in the pan for 20 minutes. Store in refrigerator 24 hours before slicing.

Banana Bread — Yields 12–14 slices

1 cup sugar
½ cup shortening
2 eggs
1 cup mashed ripe bananas
1 tablespoon lemon juice
2 cups self-rising flour
1 cup chopped nuts

Cream shortening and sugar. Add eggs, lemon juice, and mashed bananas. Add flour to above mixture and mix well. Blend in nuts. Pour into greased and floured 9 × 5 × 2-inch loaf pan. Bake at 375° for one hour. Cool in pan. Do not slice for 24 hours.

Pumpkin Bread — Yields 1 large loaf

3⅓ cups plain flour
½ teaspoon baking powder
2 teaspoons soda
1 teaspoon salt
1 teaspoon cinnamon
½ teaspoon cloves
⅔ cup nuts
⅔ cup raisins
2⅔ cups sugar
⅔ cup salad oil
4 eggs
2 cups canned pumpkin
⅔ cup water

Sift dry ingredients together. Toss nuts and fruits lightly into flour mixture. Beat sugar and oil in mixer at slow speed. Add eggs one at a time and mix well. Add flour mixture and water and mix on medium speed for 3 minutes. Bake at 350° for 1 hour. Slices well after 24 hours.

Cranberry Nut Bread — Yields 1 large loaf

1 cup sugar
2 cups self-rising flour
1 teaspoon baking soda
1 egg
¼ cup vegetable oil
¾ cup orange juice
1 tablespoon grated orange rind
1 cup chopped fresh cranberries
½ cup finely chopped pecans

Mix dry ingredients. Beat egg and mix with oil, juice, and orange rind. Add liquid to dry ingredients, stirring just enough to moisten. Fold in cranberries and nuts. Bake in greased large loaf pan for 50 minutes at 350° or until toothpick inserted comes out clean. Store for 24 hours before slicing.

SWEET TIDBITS

Apricot Balls — Yields 48 balls

1 12-ounce box dried apricots
Juice of 1 lemon
2 cups shredded coconut
½ cup sweetened condensed milk
Powdered sugar

Process apricots in food processor until finely chopped. Mix apricots, coconut, and lemon juice. Add condensed milk to bind mixture together. Shape into balls using about 1½ teaspoons for each. Roll in powdered sugar. Chill.

Banana-Split Cake — Serves 20

1 12-ounce bag vanilla wafers
¾ cup melted margarine
2 cups powdered sugar
1 cup softened margarine
5 sliced bananas
1 20-ounce can crushed pineapple, drained
1 large carton whipped topping
1 cup chopped nuts
Maraschino cherry halves

Crush vanilla wafers and combine with melted margarine. Press into 13 × 9 × 2-inch pan. Combine powdered sugar and butter and spread over crumb crust. Layer other ingredients as follows: sliced bananas, crushed pineapple, whipped topping, chopped nuts. Garnish with maraschino cherry halves. Cut into 20 party size servings.

Butterscotch Brownies — Yields 48 1½-inch squares

1 stick margarine softened
2 cups firmly packed dark brown sugar
2 eggs
1 teaspoon vanilla
1 cup plain flour
1 6-ounce package semisweet chocolate chips
1 cup nuts, chopped

Mix margarine and brown sugar and stir together over low heat until completely mixed. Allow to cool. Add eggs, vanilla, and flour and blend thoroughly. Blend in chocolate chips and chopped nuts. Turn mixture into 9 × 12-inch pan and bake in oven at 350° for about 20 minutes or until crust has formed on top of the brownies. Cut into small squares while still warm.

Chapel Window Cookies — Yields 36 slices

¼ pound margarine
1 12-ounce bag chocolate chips
1 10-ounce bag multicolored mini marshmallows
1 cup chopped nuts
1 8-ounce package chopped coconut

Melt margarine and chocolate chips in double boiler. Cool slightly, then stir in nuts and marshmallows. Spread coconut on a large sheet of waxed paper. Spoon first mixture onto coconut and roll into a long log, adding coconut if necessary to coat outside of log. Wrap in waxed paper and refrigerate or freeze until ready to serve. Slice into ½-inch slices.

Coconut Toast Fingers — Yields 48 fingers

12 slices white bread, crusts removed
1 12-ounce can sweetened condensed milk
1 6-ounce package grated coconut

Cut each slice of bread into 4 fingers. Dip each finger into condensed milk, then roll in coconut. Place on a cookie sheet and bake in oven at 400° for 6–8 minutes or until coating is light brown.

Fruitcake Cookies — Yields about 50 cookies

1½ cups self-rising flour
½ teaspoon baking soda
½ teaspoon cinnamon
½ cup brown sugar, firmly packed
2 eggs
¼ cup milk
3 cups candied mixed fruit
3 cups chopped nuts

Mix dry ingredients. Cream brown sugar and butter. Add eggs and mix well. Add dry ingredients and milk alternately, mixing well after each addition. Fold in fruits and nuts. Drop by teaspoon onto lightly greased cookie sheet. Bake in oven at 350° for 10 minutes or until lightly brown.

Fruit Pizza — Yields 1 12-inch pizza

1 roll sugar cookie dough
1 cup prepared white icing
½ teaspoon red food coloring
1 cup crushed pineapple, drained
1 cup mandarin orange sections, drained
1 cup sliced strawberries

Roll cookie dough into a 12-inch circle and bake on a pizza pan until lightly brown. Remove giant cookie to decorative serving plate and build pizza as follows: Color the icing with food coloring and spread over cookie. Spread a layer of crushed pineapple. Arrange mandarin orange sections randomly over pineapple. Garnish with sliced strawberries. Cut into triangles, pizza style except smaller.

Mincemeat Tarts — Yields 24 small tarts

Purchase bakery miniature tart shells or bake your own, using basic pastry dough and tiny tart shell pans.

Mincemeat Filling

½ cup sugar
½ stick margarine
2 eggs
1 cup mincemeat

Cream sugar and margarine. Add beaten eggs. Mix well. Add mincemeat and mix lightly. Spoon into tart shells and bake in oven at 300° for 25 minutes or until filling is set. If desired, top with a teaspoon of whipped cream or whipped topping.

Lemon Pecan Balls — Yields 36 1-inch balls

½ cup confectioners sugar
½ cup margarine
1 teaspoon lemon extract
1 cup plain flour
1 cup finely chopped pecans
Pinch of salt if desired
Confectioners sugar for coating

Cream the sugar and butter until smooth. Add lemon extract and mix well. Add flour, nuts, and salt if desired. Refrigerate dough for at least one hour. Shape into 1-inch balls and place on cookie sheet. Bake in oven at 350° for 12 minutes or until lightly brown. While still warm, roll balls in confectioners sugar and cool on wire rack. Keeps well if stored in airtight container.

Chocolate Peanut Butter Softies — Yields 50 cookies

¾ cup brown sugar, firmly packed
½ cup peanut butter
1 stick margarine
1 egg
1 teaspoon vanilla
1½ cups self-rising flour
50 small milk chocolate kisses

Combine first 3 ingredients and mix well. Add egg and vanilla. Blend in flour, stirring until all ingredients are mixed. Refrigerate dough for at least 1 hour. Shape dough into 1-inch balls and place on ungreased cookies sheets. Bake in oven at 350° for 5 minutes. Remove from oven and place a chocolate kiss in center of each. Return to oven and bake for 3 more minutes. Do not overcook. Cool completely and store in airtight containers.

Punch Bowl Cake — Serves 20–24

1 box yellow cake mix
2 3¾-ounce packages instant vanilla pudding
Milk as directed for preparing pudding
2 #2½ cans pineapple chunks, undrained
2 #2½ cans cherry pie filling
1 large container nondairy whipped topping
1 cup finely chopped nuts

Bake cake as directed. Cool. Prepare pudding as directed. Layer ingredients in a large punch bowl as follows: cake, pineapple, pudding, cherry pie filling, whipped topping. Repeat these layers. Top with nuts. Refrigerate until serving time. Serve with ladle into sherbet dishes.

Scripture Fruit Cake — Yields 1 large cake

NOTE: Some scripture references are somewhat vague.

1 cup butter (Judg. 5:25)
3 cups sugar (Jer. 6:20)
6 eggs (Isa. 10:14)
3½ cups flour (1 Kings 4:22)
⅛ teaspoon salt (Lev. 2:13)
1 cup water (Prov. 25:21) or 1 cup wine (1 Tim. 5:23)
2 cups raisins (1 Sam. 30:12)
2 cups figs (1 Sam. 30:12)
1 cup almonds (Num. 17:8)
¼ cup honey (Gen. 43:11)
1 cup nuts (Gen. 43:11)
Spices as desired (1 Kings 10:10)

Cream butter and sugar. Add eggs and mix well. Add salt to flour. Add this mixture alternately with the water or wine, mixing after each addition. When batter is well mixed, add other ingredients, mixing lightly after each ingredient is added. Bake in a slow oven at 300° (Lev. 2:4) for 1 hour and 20 minutes or until cake feels firm and begins to pull away from pan. Frost with caramel icing if desired.

NOTE: This cake is a conversation piece for any church function, especially if the recipe is made available either with the actual ingredients or just the scripture references.

Sugar Cookies — Yields 3 dozen medium cookies

2 sticks margarine
1 cup oil
1 cup granulated sugar
1 cup powdered sugar
2 eggs
4 cups plain flour
1 teaspoon soda
1 teaspoon salt
1 teaspoon cream of tartar
1 teaspoon vanilla

Cream first 4 ingredients. Add eggs. Combine next four ingredients and mix well with the sugar, oil, and egg mixture. Add vanilla. Drop with a teaspoon onto a greased cookie sheet. Flatten each cookie with a glass dipped in granulated sugar. Bake in oven at 350° for 10 minutes or until lightly browned. Do not overbake.

Stained-Glass Window Cake — Yields 16–20 slices

2 3-ounce packages strawberry gelatin
1 3-ounce package lime gelatin
3 cups boiling water
1½ cups cold water
1 3-ounce package lemon gelatin
1 cup boiling water
½ cup pineapple juice
1½ cups graham cracker crumbs
⅓ cup melted margarine
2 3-ounce packages cream cheese
¼ cup milk

Prepare strawberry and lime gelatin separately, using 1 cup boiling water and ½ cup cold water for each package. Pour each mixture into an 8 × 8-inch pan. Chill until firm and cut into ½-inch cubes.

After above step is finished, combine lemon gelatin and 1 cup boiling water. Stir until dissolved. Add pineapple juice and chill until slightly thickened. Meanwhile, mix the crumbs and melted butter and press into a 9-inch spring-form pan.

Mix cream cheese with milk and blend into lemon gelatin mixture. Fold in firm red and green gelatin cubes and pour mixture into prepared pan. Chill at least 5 hours. Loosen sides from pan with a thin knife and unmold. Slice and serve garnished with whipped topping if desired.

Tiny Cream Puffs — Yields 40–50 puffs

⅓ cup margarine
1 cup boiling water
1 cup plain flour
⅛ teaspoon salt
4 eggs

Combine butter and boiling water in a sauce pan. Add flour and salt and mix well. Cook over low heat, stirring constantly with a wooden spoon until mixture begins to pull away from the sides of the pan and forms a smooth, compact mass. Remove from heat and allow to cool about 2 minutes. Add 4 unbeaten eggs one at a time, beating vigorously after each egg is added. Drop by small teaspoons onto greased cookie sheet. Bake in oven at 400° for 10 minutes, then reduce heat to 350° for 10–20 minutes or until golden brown and set. Cool. Slit top of each puff and fill.

MEAT VARIATION: Fill with tuna fish or crab meat for a delicious change. Serve as tea sandwiches.

Chocolate Cream Puff Filling — Yields 1½ cups

12 ounces semisweet chocolate
1 6-ounce carton whipping cream

Chop chocolate into small pieces in saucepan. Add the cream and cook over medium heat until cream is warm and chocolate is melted. Stir until mixture is very smooth and allow to stand at room temperature until ready to fill puffs.

Cherry Cream Puff Filling — Yields 1½ cups

1 6-ounce carton whipping cream
1 cup confectioners sugar
1 tablespoon maraschino cherry juice
½ cup chopped maraschino cherries

Blend sugar into cream. Add cherries and juice. Stir until smooth and even colored. Fill cream puffs.

MISCELLANEOUS PARTY FOODS

Cheese Biscuits — Yields 36 small biscuits

2 cups sharp cheddar cheese, grated
2 cups self-rising flour
¼ teaspoon hot pepper sauce
¼ teaspoon Worcestershire sauce
1 stick margarine, softened

Combine all ingredients, adding margarine after others have been mixed. Roll out to ¼-inch thick and cut with small biscuit cutter. Bake in oven at 350° for 10–12 minutes. Keeps well for several weeks in an airtight container.

Curried Cashew Nuts — Serves 24

2 pounds raw cashew nuts
¼ cup vegetable oil
Curry powder
Black pepper

Sauté cashew nuts in oil until golden brown. Drain on paper towels and sprinkle lightly with curry powder and black pepper. Toss to mix flavors.

Ham and Cheese Balls — Yields 16 balls (1 t. each)

1 4-ounce can deviled ham
1 6-ounce package cream cheese
1 cup pecan meal or finely chopped pecans

Process ham and cheese in food processor until mixed well. Chill. Shape into small balls and roll in pecan meal or chopped pecans. Serve with wooden picks.

Mints

½ stick margarine
¼ cup white corn syrup
¼ teaspoon salt
1¼–1½ pounds confectioners sugar, sifted
½ teaspoon mint extract
¼ teaspoon green food color

Combine margarine, corn syrup, and salt. Add sugar, mint extract, and food color. Mix into a smooth, firm mass. (Additional sugar may be needed to reach desired consistency.) Shape into patties and place on a cookie sheet to dry and become firm. Store in airtight container in cool place.

Nuts and Bolts

1 12-ounce package red Spanish Peanuts
1 cup pecan halves
4 cups thin pretzels
4 cups each of bite-size wheat, oat and rice cereals
2 sticks margarine
1 tablespoon Worcestershire sauce
¼ teaspoon red pepper sauce
1 tablespoon garlic powder

Mix nuts and cereals in a large roasting pan. Mix remaining ingredients and heat until well mixed. Pour over cereals and mix well. Bake in oven at 200° for 1½ hours, stirring every 15 minutes.

Salted Pecans

1 pound whole pecan halves
½ cup margarine melted
Salt as desired

Place pecan halves in large shallow pan. Pour melted margarine over nuts. Sprinkle with salt. Cook in oven at 350° for 20 minutes, stirring often. Drain on paper towels. Nuts should be crisp and golden brown.

VARIATION: Use recipe for Ham and Cheese Balls. Make a sandwich using two pecan halves and a half teaspoon of ham cheese mixture.

Sausage Balls — Yields 60 balls (2 t. each)

1 pound hot pork sausage
½ pound grated sharp cheddar cheese
2 cups biscuit mix

Mix together and roll into 1-inch balls. Cook on lightly greased cookie sheet for 12–15 minutes or until lightly browned.

Stuffed Celery

Buy tender celery hearts. Wash and cut into 1½-inch pieces. Chill until very crisp. Fill with deli-prepared pimiento cheese filling.

INDEX

ADDITIONAL RECIPES